CHANGE
IS AN
INSIDE
JOB

by
Gordon Graham

Author of
The One Eyed Man is King

Published by Gordon Graham &
Company, Seattle, Washington.

Cover illustration by Todd Arbuckle
of Ego Design, Inc., Bellevue, WA

This book is dedicated to the champions of change: all the men and women in corporations, unions, government agencies, inner cities and prisons, who work to make life better for human kind.

ABOUT THE AUTHOR

Gordon Graham is a powerful, electrifying speaker on change and its impact on people. Gordon has been involved in staff and inmate training/education in correctional institutes across the United States and Canada for the past twenty-five years. His program, *A Framework for Breaking Barriers* is credited with changing the entire culture in some of the toughest prisons in the country. *Framework for Change 2000* uses the same concepts to create positive change in corporations all across America. Gordon's programs provide inspiration and hope for people in many settings: correctional institutions, government agencies, private industries and organizations of all sizes.

Gordon Graham & Company has produced the following video-taped training programs:

A Framework for Breaking Barriers
A Framework for Recovery
Safety Plus
A Framework for Change 2000
Bridges
On Solid Ground

If you'd like more information, please call 1-800-875-3530.

Contents

Acknowledgements

There are so many people who have played a part in this book. To try and acknowledge each one would be impossible. General Motors and the United Auto Workers' Union, Merck Pharmaceutical and the O.C.A.W., Union Pacific Railroad, American Commercial Barge Lines, Trendwest, Eagle Crest, and John Deere Tractor are but a few of the companies and corporations who have opened their doors to me. In Corrections, the numbers are too great to list: Oregon, Idaho, California, Missouri, Virginia, Iowa, and Wisconsin have all opened the doors of their prisons and allowed me to bring a message of hope and change to the men and women locked in their institutions. The corporate and union leaders know who they are, but I want to acknowledge their dedication to improving the lives of their employees. Corrections staffs, from directors to line staff who still believe that change is possible, have opened doors for offenders to participate in a process that can have a dramatic impact on their lives. I want to acknowledge their courage at a time when there is little support for the idea of change. I also want to acknowledge the inmates in prisons across the country who facilitate the change process so that other inmates in their institutions can return to their communities better equipped to become productive members of society.

I'd like to share a story with you. A guy working for General Motors took early retirement with a buyout of eighty thousand dollars. Before he started his new life, he decided to go out to Las Vegas for a short vacation. He purchased a round trip airline ticket and flew to Vegas. He was a gambler, and decided to shoot some dice. He got on the craps table and began to lose. This losing streak continued until he was flat broke. He still had his plane ticket left, but before he left the casino, he needed to use the restroom. To his dismay, he realized that it would require a quarter to enter a restroom stall. He was broke and didn't even have a quarter. He turned to another gentleman in the restroom and, in embarrassment, asked if he could borrow a quarter. "If you'll give me your business card, I'll send you the quarter when I get back to Detroit," he reassured him. The guy said, "Don't be silly, here's a quarter." But after further insistence, the guy handed him his business card. When he turned and walked over to the toilet, he realized that the stall door was open. He used the toilet, and when he came out, the man who had lent him the quarter was already gone. He started to leave the casino and, walking past a row of quarter machines, dropped the quarter into one, pulled the handle, and hit a one hundred-dollar jackpot. He took the hundred dollars and went back to the dice table. His luck turned, and he won all his money back. He went back to Detroit, went into business for himself, and became very successful. A few years later he was telling a friend about his experience in Las Vegas. "The thing that has always bothered me is that I've never been able to thank that guy." His friend said, "I thought he gave you his business card." He responded, "Oh, that's not the guy I wanted to thank; it's the guy who left the door open for me!"

We all have a responsibility to leave the door open for our children and grandchildren. I have a responsibility to leave the door open for people like me. I want to acknowledge the men and women who work to open doors, and leave them open for other people.

I also want to thank Pat Jusich for her editorial assistance and for her dedication to keeping me focused. Her creative ideas helped me to finally complete this project. I also want to thank Annette Bessey for her willingness to spend many days, and into the nights putting all of my ramblings into a computer, and then bringing it out so that it made some sense.

Also, a special thanks to my wife, Eve, for her feedback and willingness to listen to each new chapter, and for her love and support during this writing project.

Gordon Graham

Foreword:
Change is an inside job...

In 1971, a man named Gordon Graham, who had spent the better part of his life behind bars, walked out of Walla Walla State Prison determined to stay out. He had never made it for very long on the outside before, but this time would be different. This time he would change.

Today, some 27 years later, Gordon Graham is a successful, highly respected advisor to leaders in both the public and private sectors; a published author and sought-after speaker; and creator of a series of dynamic training programs that have helped thousands of people from all walks of life create meaningful, positive change in their own lives.

His personal transformation is the stuff of fiction; but everyone who has ever met him face to face, or heard him speak in public, or even seen him on videotape knows that this man is real. When he says, "If *I* could change, *anyone* can change!" they believe him. And time and time again, using the principles he teaches, they go on to prove it in their own lives.

Gordy -- as everyone calls him -- reaches people in a profound and very personal way. To meet him is to be immediately affected. To participate in one of his programs is to suddenly see things from a whole new perspective. And to be his friend is a constantly surprising experience. He has devoted every ounce of his energy to bringing the change concepts to prisons throughout this country and Canada — for those who run them and those who are incarcerated in them. The impact his programs have made on individuals and entire correctional systems is incalculable.

Few people can attest to this more personally than Jim Harris who met Gordy near the end of his own 17-year sentence in a California prison. Harris was a leader with considerable influence in his particular yard.

"When Gordy talked, I began seeing things for the first time. He explained that a current reality is where you are, and a vision is where you want to be. Well, my current reality was I was in prison, and my vision was that I never wanted to come back. Going through the process with the tools he laid out, I could see that I was never going to have to come back."

Jim Harris' story is not an isolated one. David Lewis was a Black Guerilla Gang leader in San Quentin and Folsom prisons. Out on parole and enrolled in a state-mandated drug and alcohol treatment facility, Lewis first met Gordon Graham on videotape.

"After four sessions of Breaking Barriers, it was like I was opened up enough to accept what was coming out of this guy's mouth. He didn't look like me, but he sounded like I felt."

Today, David is the Chairman of the Board of Free at Last, an organization that is successfully bringing positive change, jobs, and a new self-image to East Palo Alto, California, a community that was once known as the murder capital of the world. In 1995, David was awarded the California Peace Prize for his work in East Palo Alto.

Gordy's commitment to changing the prison culture, from administrators to inmates, is unquestioned. But he is also no stranger to the world of big business. This man who can get prison guards and inmates together in a room without rancor is also known for doing the same thing with business executives and labor leaders.

A case in point is his long-standing involvement with General Motors Corporation. Jay Wilber, Executive Director-Quality Network for GM, has worked with Gordy for years and is particularly impressed with his ability to connect with management, union leaders, and line employees with equal credibility.

Ed Vallo, President of O.C.A.W. Union 88-580, heard Gordy speak at a conference years ago in Washington, D.C. He came away feeling that everyone in a union, regardless of their position, should sit down and listen to this man. His organization has certainly done that, instituting *A Framework for Change* as part of its goal-sharing program and witnessing changes across the board in every department.

"The things he went through may be different from ours, but we are all affected by our experiences. Every day, we are faced with problems, whether they are in our personal life or our work life. Gordy just presents a unique way of dealing with those problems. You wonder sometimes how you were dealing with things before Gordy came into your life."

Gordy's ability to relate to people from all backgrounds is a most unusual trait and one that stems directly from growing up in a prison environment, in the opinion of Gregg Ganschaw. Ganschaw, a master facilitator of Gordy's programs, believes the secret lies in getting beyond fear.

"Gordy has looked fear in the face so often that he's just gotten past it. He's able to be genuine, without carrying around the doubts that most of us have. Once you get to that point, you can tell it like it is no matter who you're talking to."

Jerry Andres, long-time friend and CEO of Eagle Crest Group, reports overwhelming acceptance of Gordy's programs among his staff in Redmond, Oregon.

"He approaches problems that have been the nemesis of a lot of CEOs. He bridges gaps that occur between senior management and the workforce. You don't get invited back to clients unless you are delivering the goods. Gordy's programs have delivered. We've brought in other programs, but not on any permanent basis. Framework for Change is a way of life here at

Eagle Crest; it's how we conduct our business."

Gordon Graham is a man with a mission; to convince people that change is possible; that they have the power to bring it about in their own lives; and that there are learnable, practical ways to do that. Every presentation he gives, every program he facilitates, every conversation he engages in underscores those fundamental ideas.

Make no mistake, Gordon Graham is a singular individual with a powerful message — a message that transcends race, gender, age, ethnic background, education, economic or social status. The message is simply this: "If you want to change, you can. But it's up to *you* to make it happen."

Bobbi Linkemer

Bobbi Linkemer, a long-time friend of Gordon Graham, is an author and the owner of a business communications consulting firm.

Part One

1. From Out Of The Shadows

"Ex-Con Inspires Others to Change." The article from the *St. Louis Post Dispatch* had been faxed to my office in Seattle.

I'd just returned from the General Motors Plant in Arlington, Texas where I'd been conducting a three-day workshop on *A Framework for Change*. It had been a month since I'd been in St. Louis and I'd forgotten all about the interview. The article mentioned that an ex-con was in St. Louis to conduct a seminar for the business community on how to manage change. It talked of the man's work with General Motors and the United Auto Workers and his involvement with prisons across the United States.

It was actually a very positive article, but the headline took me by surprise. "Ex-con" it said. I thought, "Damn! I've been out of prison twenty-four years! I'm a father, grandfather, business owner, husband, respected trainer, educator, and taxpayer. I've been granted a full pardon, but the one part of who I am that sells papers is the 'ex-con' label." I wonder how many people can't get beyond that label? How many people live in the shadows of the past, afraid to let others see who they really are, because they fear they won't be accepted? How many people stay locked inside their own prisons because they don't, or can't, believe that change is possible?

I've been teaching and writing on change since 1973. This book, *Change is an Inside Job*, is meant to help the reader get a glimpse of how change can and does alter the internal image of an individual. It's a challenge to step out of the shadows. The past is always there, hidden in the corners of our mind, invisible at times. But, when the individual is faced with a specific issue or challenge, the shadows of the past are illuminated and we are forced to relive old experiences that have long been buried in our minds. Sometimes the old patterns become so much a part of who we are that, when they surface, it's hard for us to recognize the old behavior.

I'd been out of prison for twenty-five years and was the owner of a small training company. My computer system needed to be upgraded to respond to the needs of my office staff. A good friend recommended a computer consultant that he had used. I called and set up an appointment and decided to contract with the individual to upgrade our systems. He asked me to advance him $7,500 to buy parts, etc., and because he was self-employed, I did. Time passed and he continued to procrastinate on providing the services. When this continued, I asked one of my associates to check on the guy and find out a little more about his reputation. We discovered that he had used the same scam on a large number of other small companies like my own. My accountant and my wife, who happened to be the president of our company, asked me to call the police. I grew up in a world where you didn't snitch — where you didn't call The Man on other people. Until this situation surfaced, I never realized how deeply that principle had been driven into my system. I couldn't bring myself to call the police. I told my accountant and my wife that either of them could call the police, but that I wouldn't do it. After that experience, I had to go back and reevaluate that old piece of my past and ask myself if that principle was still relevant. Obviously, the answer is "no." I had a responsibility to my fellow citizens to protect them from this type of individual. But I had never had to face this issue before even though it lay hidden in the deep recesses of my mind.

Over the years I've overcome hundreds of similar principles that came from my past. I've had to make a lot of choices. The past can be a heavy anchor that holds us back, or we can use the past as a springboard into the future, freeing ourselves from the prisons we have created in our minds.

When we turn from the past and look to the future, many of our old experiences can be strengths that allow us to more effectively reach our future goals. My early life on the streets and my experiences as a consumer of correctional services have given me the empathy and understanding that allows me to bridge the gap between inmates and staff and unions and management. Many of the skills that I learned on the streets and in prisons transferred into an honest framework and have become great assets. My friend, David Lewis, a former Black Guerilla Gang leader, has been able to utilize many of the skills that made him a gang leader in bringing about constructive change in communities. We need to learn from the past and then turn it loose and move to the future.

"The past is history, the future is a mystery, but the present belongs to me!"

This is a book about change. It explores the many aspects of change up close and personal. Some people manage to overcome seemingly impossible odds. What are the common threads that run through their thought patterns? Is change possible? Are there tools that can be taught and internalized by the student? Can you teach an old dog new tricks? What techniques and processes are necessary to support and reinforce positive change? How do you overcome the barriers from the past and move forward to an exciting future? My goal is to show people how to emerge from the shadows and find the freedom that comes from discovering who they really are.

To do a credible job of writing about change, let's go back to the beginning. Back to the cellblocks, back to the streets and the experiences that molded the self-image of a convict.

When I look back through my life with an awareness of the change process, I can see the traps I was caught up in with clarity. I entered prison as a naïve, scared young man. I had my first experience with a strip search. "Bend over and spread your cheeks", the guard barked. Disinfectant was sprayed over my body, saturating my hair. With coveralls and a bedroll that consisted of a paper-thin blanket and a mattress not much thicker than the blanket, I was herded into a cellblock, paraded down a tier and finally locked in a 6' by 10' cell. This was the start of a twenty-year career that spawned an archetypal convict.

When I first entered prison, it was not my intent to become a convict. I wanted out! The prison environment is a world with its own value system, a world where might makes right. I was forced to accept the reality that I was no longer a part of society. I forfeited all rights to dignity and justice. Somehow my self-image adjusted and I gradually began to develop survival skills. The fear subsided and I began to establish a new identity. The more time I did, the easier it was to function in the prison environment. The more I adjusted to prison, the more difficult it was to make it on the outside. Gradually, I became disconnected from society and became a part of the prison subculture. When I left prison I no longer fit in society; I felt alienated.

For years I felt as though God had left a component out of me. I'd see other people who were successful and I wanted whatever it was they had, but I didn't know how to get from where I was to where I wanted to be.

For the inmate, the pressure of the prison culture is seven days a week, twenty-four hours each day. There is no escape, no refuge from the prison mentality. To deviate or forget where you are could have serious, life-threatening consequences. A friendly discussion with "The Man," who represented anyone with any authority, could seriously impact your status as a "good convict". A sign of weakness or an emotional breakdown could cause ridicule from your cellmates, or from guards. To even consider informing on a fellow convict, regardless of the cruelty or insanity of their act, would be suicide. To suggest that there was something wrong with stealing or using drugs would open you to abuse by your peers. So, gradually and incrementally the individual buys into and accepts the unwritten rules of the society they're part of.

When I tell people about my first experience in prison, it is not to elicit anyone's sympathy, nor do I want to relate a "poor me" story. I was what I was then, and I am what I am now. My purpose in taking the reader back to the cell blocks of Monroe Reformatory is to use that set of experiences to demonstrate the impact that incremental change has on all our lives. We are all unique beings, so my experience may not accurately describe every inmate's perception of how the prison culture alters the individual's picture of reality. However, after forty-five years of interacting with staff and inmates in prisons across the United States, there are too many similarities in the stories of others with my background for it not to have some validity.

To call Monroe a Reformatory is a misnomer of the highest magnitude. It was a prison then and still is to this day. I entered Monroe in 1951, young, scared and alone. I'd been sentenced to twenty years for first degree forgery in the small town of Wenatchee, Washington. After sentencing, I was transferred from the county jail to the prison in a green bullet-shaped van with the infamous title, "The Green Hornet". The trip from the county jail to Monroe was a degrading experience in itself. However it wasn't a deterrent. After my first release, I continued down the same path and rode the Green Hornet back to Monroe and eventually to Walla Walla, Washington's maximum security prison, the end of the line in the prison system.

The intake process at Monroe consisted of mug shots, fingerprints, strip searching, spraying with disinfectant, blue jeans and a denim shirt, a bed roll, and a liberal dose of "thou shalts" and "thou shalt nots." They threw in a sprinkling of information about your ancestors just to make sure you were now ready to enter prison.

The cellblock was huge. The catwalks that ran in front of the long rows of cells seemed to go on forever. The air was warm and heavy with the strong, pungent smell of antiseptic. Gray cement floors were still wet with dirty streaks of water from their morning scrubbing. The cells that looked like long rows of apple boxes standing on end had gray steel bars across the front, like cages.

We shuffled along the corridor of the cellblock, dressed in our state-issued, ill-fitting blue denim outfits. An inmate dressed in form-fitting khakis lounged against the door of the first cell on the tier. He eyed us coldly as we passed by.

As we marched along we were greeted by cat calls; lewd invitations and a litany of descriptions about our future in "The Joint." None were positive. New arrivals were referred to as "fish" and were housed in the "fish tank." Prisons have their own pecking order and the "fish" are at the bottom of the hierarchy. If you're a "first timer" it can be a brutal introduction to the prison environment.

I later realized that anger and hostility are learned behaviors that serve as defense mechanisms for prisoners caught up in a system that perpetuates failure.

"Open'em up," the guard with us yelled.

The khaki-clad inmate reached over and slowly pulled a long lever, and the narrow, barred doors of the individual cells slid noisily open.

"What's happening?"

"The new fish get in?"

"Any pretty ones?"

"I get first choice."

The voices of unseen faces sounded hollow as they echoed through the huge dungeon-like cellblock.

"Okay, let's go!" the guard yelled as he moved down the line of cells. He began to call out names followed by the cell number that was printed over each of the narrow openings. As each name was called, one of the inmates stepped through the cell door and steel against steel signaled the end as the door slammed behind him.

I was the third name called.

"Graham, 9-A."

I shifted my roll of blankets in my arms and walked slowly into the tiny cubicle. It was so narrow you could stand in the middle of it, hold your arms out, and touch both sides with your fingertips. There was a thin, well-used mattress stretched out on a decrepit army cot against one side of the cell. A small sink with most of the enamel worn away was attached to the back wall next to a toilet stained and chipped from years of use.

"You can't even take a sh— in private!" I thought. It seemed like a final insult to my dignity.

The only other furnishing was a small wooden stool that now served as a table for the brown paper bag that held my worldly possessions.

The cell door slid shut behind me with the loud clang of metal against metal.

I felt totally alone. The feeling of loneliness was so overwhelming it was almost suffocating. I sat down on the cot and rubbed my face with both hands. Silently I cried out, "If there's a God, why am I here?" I'd never needed so much to believe in God. I felt utter helplessness, as if I was at the mercy of this stark, monstrous cellblock. There's a feeling of finality when you enter a prison! Until the cell door closes, there's still a glimmer of hope that some miracle, a national emergency, a benefactor, God, will come free you. But, when the steel doors slam shut, it's a reality – you're now a prisoner.

The noise of doors banging and discordant voices ricocheting off walls up and down the long cavernous cellblock became almost unbearable. I covered my ears with my hands and thought, "Why me? This couldn't be happening to me; not for a lousy hundred-and-fifty-dollar check that I forged. Damn that judge! Damn that prosecutor!" I let that sheriff talk me into pleading guilty and I believed him when he told me I wouldn't do more than a year in the reformatory. In court I'd pleaded guilty to all charges. The judge, without even batting an eye, sentenced me to twenty years. Twenty years? I was naïve. I had no awareness of the sentencing structure. Twenty years was a lifetime.

"Yes, son, twenty years, but you probably won't do any more than a year to fifteen months, depending on what the parole board decides." The Judge was trying to ease my panic, but all I could hear was "twenty years."

I had been duped. I was guilty, but I had been duped. This was the beginning of a long downward spiral into the world of prisons, parole, escapes, and failure. It was twenty years later before I managed to see the other side of darkness.

The worst prisons in the world are the ones we lock ourselves in. The tragedy is when we hold the key and either can't find it, or fail to use it.

It didn't take me long to discover the realities at Monroe. The internal functions of the institution were controlled by the strongest inmates. Everything had a price. You had to pay to get any of the meaningful work assignments. If you wanted a decent cell, you had to pay for it. Convict cliques used strong-arm tactics and operated with immunity. It was a corrupt culture.

I didn't know anyone in Monroe so I became subject to all of the games convicts play. I just wanted to do my time. I wanted out; I wanted to become a part of the real world. My thoughts were on how stupid I had been to wind up in prison. I wanted to get out, get a job, find a nice lady, settle down and get a handle on my life. I wanted the same things that every human being wants. I wanted to be safe, to be loved, to be treated with respect, to be valued and to be free. However, these thoughts got lost in the struggle for survival inside the prison. The prison culture sucks the beauty of life from your soul and gradually and incrementally you become callous and insensitive to the indignities which are daily events in a prison environment.

My adjustment to prison life was a difficult, painful education. I wasn't in prison a full day before I was challenged by the internal hierarchy. A convict who was part of one of the cliques that had gotten used to bullying new arrivals stole my shoes. I broke his nose before "The Man" could pull me off, and as a result I got my first introduction to The Hole. The captain of the guards sentenced me to ten days in The Hole on bread and water. Bread and water turned out to be "fritters", a soggy vegetable patty stuffed between two slices of white bread. I felt I had been justified in defending my property; being sentenced to The Hole just reinforced my belief that the system was corrupt.

This first altercation in the prison got me labeled as a troublemaker by both staff and inmates. For the next year I became a regular in The Hole. I was in constant conflict with both the guards and other inmates. Fights and rule infractions became the norm. I learned how to do time in The Hole, and with each trip I became more of a convict. Many of the things that turned my stomach when I first arrived were becoming less offensive to me. I had adjusted to the vulgarities, the constant sexual innuendoes between convicts, the insensitivity of both staff and inmates and I could play the dozens (put-downs) and talk about your mama with the best of them. Hell, I was becoming a convict. My final indoctrination came as a result of a prison riot.

It was a hot August afternoon. The prison yard was open for our evening exercise time. Three hundred or so inmates were engaged in a variety of time-killing activities trying to survive the sweltering heat. A softball game was underway and two or three guys were playing handball. Most of the cons were just following the shade that stretched out from the base of the prison wall. There were small groups sprawled on the ground playing cards and dominoes. Some were talking about their exploits on the streets or just daydreaming about what life could be. On the surface it was a typical prison yard-out.

But, there was an underlying tension that had been building for months. The prison administration had allowed the corrupt practices to spread until it was like a festering sore and many of the inmates who were victims of the system had been talking about some kind of protest.

The prison yard had ball fields and recreational areas, as well as a brick mill, the education building, a cannery, and the powerhouse. There was a twenty-two foot brick wall that surrounded the area with gun towers in each corner where guards could survey the inmates' activities on the yard.

I'd been walking around the yard with one of the guys who had spent a lot of time in The Hole with me. We were just kicking ideas around on how to beat the Joint when he said, "Man this Joint is gonna' blow wide open one of these days!" My walking partner had been in and out of Monroe for the last ten years and he was aware of most of the things going on inside The Walls. I knew there was a lot of hostility among the convicts and it was common knowledge that the administration was corrupt. It was just beginning to cool off in the yard when the tower guard called, "Yard in!" "Man, just when it cools off they run us back into those cell blocks. It's like going into a f — ing oven," my partner was saying. Then someone yelled, "I ain't goin' in. F — em!" "Let's all stay in the yard", someone else yelled. "Everyone move to the gate. It's yard-in!" The microphone sounded loud. Convicts were milling around but nobody was moving toward the gate. I felt a chill run down my body. I could feel the tension in the yard. "Let's burn this m — f — down!" someone screamed. Convicts started to move away from the gate toward the buildings, "Yard in, yard in", the guard's voice was insistent. "Let's burn the brick mill," a convict yelled, and started running toward the wooden structure that held the dreaded brick mill where convicts were sent to work as punishment. Suddenly the yard erupted and convicts were charging the buildings. Within minutes, flames were licking at the dry tinder-like walls of the brick mill. Convicts were tearing through the educational building, and the cannery was on fire. It was instant insanity. I found myself running full speed across the yard. A prison guard who was stationed in the yard appeared in my path, and without even thinking, I lowered my shoulder and sent him sprawling in the dust.

As night set in, the prison was in flames. Convicts were still rampaging through the buildings, ripping and tearing at anything that was loose. By now the prison wall was alive with state police, local police, and prison guards. Convicts had begun assembling on the baseball field. Microphones blared from the walls with orders to stop and return to our cells. "F— you" was the constant chant from the milling convicts. Then two or three of the inmates, intoxicated by the shot of insanity that riots inject, stormed the wall with rocks and baseballs. "Get back or we'll shoot," the microphones were threatening. "Man, they ain't gonna' shoot," someone yelled just as the first gun shot sounded. "They're shooting blanks," the same insane voice screamed. From that point it was bedlam. The catwalk at the top of the wall erupted with gunfire. You could hear the bullets ricocheting off the walls as convicts dived for cover. I was stretched out by a pile of bricks and could hear bullets striking bricks all around me. Convicts were screaming, "I'm hit," but the firing continued. Finally it was over. Only one convict had been killed. Several were seriously wounded and one guy had lost his eyes.

We were stripped naked and marched into the cellblocks. This was a turning point for me. Unfortunately, it was a turn that would lead to Walla Walla and to a career as a convict leader. I was singled out as a ringleader of the riot. This was due partly to my reputation, and to the fact that I'd knocked down the guard. In fact, there were no ringleaders. The riot was simply an outburst of anger and frustration built up as a result of years of injustices. But, the system says there has got to be a leader. So, I got the honors. I was sentenced to a year in the Hole. When I came out of the Hole 365 days later, I was a fully developed convict. My reputation had grown and I was welcomed back to the main population as a convict leader.

By the time I was released from Monroe five years later, I had changed my paradigm. I thought like a convict. Hustling, stealing, and beating The Man was the game. Without a conscious decision to do so, I'd become part of a subculture. Gradually and incrementally, I'd gotten used to a way of life that would keep me trapped for the next two decades.

Incremental change can cause individuals, communities, and corporations to get used to practices and behavior that become major barriers to change. When we get used to things they become normal, accepted behavior. I was visiting a prison some years ago and the warden told me a story that illustrates this point. The prison had a large powerhouse that used oil as its energy source. He had been the warden at this institution for several weeks and every day at 3:00 in the afternoon a powerhouse whistle would sound. He asked one of his associate wardens why they blew the powerhouse whistle. The response was, "I don't know. They've always done it." He started asking around to find out why. The captain of the guard, when asked why the whistle blew every day, said, "I don't know, they've blown it ever since I've been here." He finally found a lieutenant who had been at the institution for 25 years. The lieutenant said, "Oh, that calls in the coal crew." The question was then, "What coal crew?" The lieutenant replied, "They used to fire the furnace with coal, and they would bring in train car loads of coal, park them outside the walls and take a crew of inmates out to unload them. Then at 3:00 they would blow the whistle to bring them in to count the inmates." The associate warden said, "But we haven't had coal here for 15 years. Why do they still blow the whistle?" The answer was, "I don't know." So, the warden decided to put an end to the 3:00 whistle, but when he did, the people who lived downtown were upset because everyone had gotten used to using the whistle to tell time. The question we need to ask ourselves when we begin the change process is why do we blow the whistle? Why do we do what we do? Does it still add value or bring us the rewards or satisfaction that it once did? If the answer is no, then we need to stop blowing the whistle.

Prison is a self-perpetuating system. The paradigm of prisons, guards, convicts, and society remains the same today as it was when I first entered prison forty-five years ago. The names have changed from convict to inmate, from guard to correctional officer, but the game remains the same. The paradigm that controls our prison system has the potential to bankrupt this country. There needs to be a paradigm shift, a major overhaul that frees corrections from the political process and redirects the energy and resources to the communities. We cannot continue to lock our problems away. We need to address the issues where they exist, and we need to invite those who are perceived as the problem to the

party. We need to question everything — our government, our legal system, our educational system,
even our basic system of values. We need to continue our journey to a new paradigm that supports
and reinforces positive change.

2. The Nature Of Change

Change has become the mantra for organizations, corporations, individuals, and whole communities. The speed of change continues to accelerate with no end in sight. The proliferation of downsizing, rightsizing, contracting out, merging, and plant closures has created an atmosphere of fear and uncertainty. Automation, technology, and information provide the fuel that drives this unquenchable need for change. In this seemingly endless quest to improve quality, cut costs, and increase profitability, we are faced with a paradox: We must learn to engage the hearts and minds of our employees, at the same time their numbers are being reduced and those who survive see their workloads increasing.

We are faced with the need for a new paradigm. What worked in the past is obsolete in this world of computers, faxes, e-mail, beepers, and the explosion of information via the Internet. This is an age of opportunity for those who are able to stretch, learn, and take calculated risks. For those locked into old practices and unwilling to accept the need to change and adapt, it's an age of stress and resentment.

To learn is to change. Education is a process that changes the learner.
George B. Leonard, *Education & Ecstasy*, 1960.

The first step to long-term change is to understand where we are at the present time. We need to define our current reality. This is not always an easy thing to do. There are a number of reasons why we are so often unaware of the current reality of a given situation. For one thing, the hurry-up, day-planner pace of our world doesn't often provide us with enough time to sit back and take a cold, hard look at things. Secondly, we tend to avoid facing up to people or situations that we feel powerless to deal with. If we can't change it, why dwell on it? While there's some validity to that, the fact is we are often much more capable of changing a situation than we may realize. Finally, our desire to maintain a positive mental attitude often finds us holding the truth at bay. Keeping a positive mental attitude does not, however, necessitate avoiding the truth. Being truly proactive means creating a vision of how you want things to be while simultaneously dealing with them as they are.

Once we've identified the current reality, we then ask the question, "Will this serve our needs over time?" Eric Hoffer once said, "In times of change, the learners inherit the earth, while the learned find themselves well equipped to deal with a world that no longer exists." If our current reality will not serve our needs over time, we need to begin the process of change.

"I never give them hell; I just tell the truth, and they think it's hell."

Harry S. Truman

This is true for us as individuals and as a part of our communities. A career path that assured long-term security is no longer a reality for this generation. Healthcare, welfare and social security are no longer guaranteed as our world changes. Bigger is no longer better and the entrepreneurial spirit has become a valuable asset in this changing world. It's an exciting time for those individuals and organizations that realize change means opportunities. However, it is a fearful future for those who try to maintain the status quo.

> **Results Take Time To Measure.**
> **GG**

This is a natural law. There's no quick fix; change is an ongoing process. Over the past 24 years, I've been involved with many corporations, companies, correctional institutions, and individuals seeking ways to change the direction of their organization and their personal lives. I've witnessed dramatic change in some corporations and individuals, and I see some who always seem to get stuck at the starting gate. It's certainly not because of a lack of information. There's a myriad of books out there that explore the process of change. Consultants, counselors and organizational development specialists can all make a case for their unique approach to the change process. In fact, the challenge of change centers around taking a concept or technique and implementing it in your organization or your life, and staying with it until it becomes integrated into your daily routine. Change is not like a car wash where you run people through a program and go back to business as usual. It takes commitment and follow-through. A common theme in organizations today is "Oh, we went through that in 19- so and so." It was the training flavor of the month. The book or theory currently in vogue swept through the industrial world like a hurricane leaving the shelves of corporate training rooms stacked with thick, three-ring binders adorned with eye-catching graphics and filled with flow charts, arrows and the profound catch phrase of some guru.

I've watched this process for the past 20 years. From large corporations to small manufacturers, the results are the same. A new training program is implemented. It shines brightly until you have trained "the choir" and then it begins to slowly fade into the archives of training history. Quality Circles, Total Quality, Quality is Free, Employee Involvement, Teams, Self-Directed Teams, Employee Empowerment, etc., etc., etc. You can change the name or package it differently, but unless you create a culture that feels ownership of the process and shares in the rewards, then it's like swimming upstream: long hours, hard work, but no progress. Broken down to their basic concepts, the messages delivered by most programs are the same. Treat all people with dignity and respect. Engage the hearts and minds of employees. Empower people to own their jobs. Expand the opportunities for employees to grow and use their talents and creativity. Reward the right things. Create a playing field where power is shared. When the organization makes money – share profits fairly. Pretty common sense stuff but it's difficult to implement if you ignore the culture of the organization.

The same process takes place in our communities. Some event or circumstance occurs that brings an awareness of the need to bring about change in a community. There is an initial focus of attention followed by a burst of energy by government agencies and social programs, but as the attention dies down, so does the energy and little is done to solve the underlying problem in the community. It takes great tenacity and a willingness to handle resistance, sometimes from the most unexpected places. People will defend the status quo even though it is destroying the community. Politics, local power brokers and financial resources become barriers to sustaining change.

The difficulty of bringing about long-term change in corporations or communities is much easier to understand when you realize how tough it is for individuals to make lasting change. New Year's resolutions, well-intentioned on January 1, become lost in the trials and tribulations of life. Most of us have started a weight loss program or resolved to save money, only to find ourselves caught up in our old practices before 30 days have gone by.

Most of us regard change as something we wish everything and everyone around us would do. We tell ourselves we'd be happy if we had more money or a nicer car, or if our spouse or children would just straighten up. In corporations, management blames the employees for the lack of success and the employees sit around and wait for management to fix things. As citizens of our communities, we blame our problems on politicians, law enforcement, or the economy in general.

There are two absolute truths about change:

•Change is not only possible, but necessary in today's world

•Change is an Inside Job.

If It's To Be, It's Up To Me!
                                        GG

Before we get into the different ways we process change, I want to talk about communication and how we sometimes impact people by the way we communicate. You and I communicate in three-dimensional form. First of all, we use words. Those words then trigger pictures. The pictures bring about a feeling or an emotional response. Sometimes, we use words that have several different meanings and the receiver sees and feels something totally different than what we intended. When I was young, if you said, "If you walk downtown dressed like that you could get stoned," it meant you'd get rocks thrown at you! Today, if you talk about getting stoned people might say, "Right on, I'll come with you." So words really have no meaning until you and I give them meaning. We need to be aware that the message we send isn't always the same as the one that's received.

I'll give you another example of missed communication. A woman who now works facilitating our programs used to work for a company that sold home improvement products. Most of the doors in the office area had signs with the letters DFWTS on them. The letters stood for (in slightly altered form) "Don't Fool With the System."

I'd be willing to bet that when the president of

the company put those signs on the doors, he did it because he truly believed that they had a foolproof system for selling their products that would lead to the sales representatives' success. Unfortunately, what it meant to the sales representatives was "management knows more than you do," "we don't trust your judgment," and "your input is not valued here."

I'm not suggesting that we need to be paranoid about everything we say, but it is worthwhile to think twice about the messages we're sending.

If you want to communicate with other people, you must have empathy. You have to crawl up inside people and see the world through their eyes. You have to put them on and wear them like a suit. Let me give you an example of empathy. I have three children. When my second daughter, Tina, was about three years old we were at a large shopping mall about three days before Christmas. The stores were crowded with people, but there were all kinds of neat Christmas decorations and Santa Clauses were doing their thing. Amidst all the festive goings-on, my Tina started to cry. I said, "Tina baby, what's wrong? It's Christmas time, look at all the neat stuff." She kept right on crying so I got down on my knees to talk to her. "Baby, what's wrong?" I asked, and I just happened to look around. What I saw was rear ends, purses and knees and it wasn't pretty at all! I thought to myself, "That's empathy." Ask yourself how it looks from the other person's viewpoint. How does it look from the point of view of the person whose job is threatened by the changes being implemented? How does change look from the perspective of the person whose skills are becoming obsolete, or the young man or woman who has been raised in a ghetto and doesn't see any opportunities? Just the word "change" frightens some people and creates excitement in others.

Change can be managed if we have an awareness of how it is mentally processed by individuals. Change is nebulous, it sneaks up on us. We have great defense mechanisms that allow us to rationalize and defend the status quo.

There are four basic ways human beings mentally process change:

•Incremental: A gradual process that allows us to adapt and get used to things.

•Pendulum: This is a short-term process and usually follows a significant emotional event.

•Change by Exception: Labeling those who do better than the norm as "exceptions". This is a natural cop-out for those who refuse to accept anything that may conflict with their picture of reality.

•Paradigm: A frame of reference that controls our decisions. A map in our minds.

We will examine these four in more depth. There are great strengths in each of the ways we process change and also great weaknesses. Our reactions to change are generally unconscious responses, therefore, awareness is the first step toward gaining control. We can't change something if we aren't aware of it. We must become aware of how change has crept up on us and we must become aware of the changes we want to make happen. Most importantly, we must become aware that we have the ability to choose how we respond to change. Once we do this, we can experience an immediate sense of freedom.

There is an old Chinese proverb that says, "A frog in a well cannot be talked to about the sea." In other words, we cannot visualize something new or different when we are locked onto the status quo. Once we learn to see outside the well, and think outside the box, we have the freedom to make virtually any change we can visualize.

Incremental Change

The first process of change that creates major challenges for individuals and for organizations is called incremental change. It is a gradual and incremental process. It sneaks up on us. One of our greatest strengths as human beings is our ability to gradually and incrementally get used to things. At first, something might bother us, but if we let it go and don't deal with the issue, whatever it is, we will gradually get used to it and it will become normal accepted behavior both individually and organizationally.

Let me share a couple of examples. We had been going through the globalization of the world for years, but in 1973 an oil cartel was formed that changed our world. Gas prices began to escalate.

About this time, I was teaching a session in Los Angeles and we were having lunch. One of the ladies at the table was complaining about the price she'd paid for gas. She said she'd paid 76 cents a gallon. Someone said, "There's talk it will be a dollar a gallon before this is over." The woman responded adamantly, "I'll never pay it! I'll ride a bicycle first!" She's not riding a bicycle, but now she's probably saying, "I'll never pay two dollars a gallon."

When we gradually and incrementally get used to things, they become our reality. We no longer see. We become blinded by our conditioning. What at first was challenging or uncomfortable becomes normal, accepted behavior. This is one of our greatest strengths, but it can also be our greatest weakness if we give up our choices and compromise our principles.

At one time in my life I was a middleweight prizefighter. I was required to weigh 160 pounds, so I was always in good physical condition. There's also pay value in being in condition if you're a fighter. If you run out of gas in the middle of a round, you can't form a committee, you can't study it; it's your rear end. When my lifestyle changed, one day I looked at the scale and I weighed 170 pounds. I thought, "Man, you'd better lose some weight." But the idea quickly passed and I got used to weighing 170. Then one day the scale read 180 pounds and I thought, "Man, you're getting heavy; you'd better do something about that weight." So, I did. I rationalized why it was okay to weigh 180. I said, "Man,

you're big boned; besides you're a manager now."
And I gradually got used to weighing 200, 210, 220.

> **The worst part of being in a rut is that
> you don't even know you're in it.**
> **GG**

We can get used to almost anything. We can get used to being miserable or unhappy. Unfortunately, people often want to share these feelings with others. We can get used to being lazy or being late. We can get used to treating people without respect, and we can get used to *being* treated without respect. When we get used to it, we are no longer aware of the behavior. The culture drives the behaviors of those who live and work in it.

While conducting a two-day seminar, at the end of the first day I suggested that people do something nice for someone that evening. The next morning one of the men came up to me and said, "Hey Gordy, you got me in trouble last night." I said, "How so?" He laughed and said, "You suggested we do something nice, so on my way home I stopped and bought my wife a bouquet of flowers. When I got home, I handed her the flowers and she said, "What have you been up to? Why are you giving me flowers? What do you want?" We both had a good laugh, but I thought, isn't it sad that we develop relationships where doing something nice for someone is suspect? In an organization, when you attempt to

involve people who heretofore have not been involved, their first question is, "Why are they inviting me? What do they want?"

Before we move to the next process of change,
this is a good time for some reflective questions.

•What have you gotten used to in areas that are
important to you? Examples: Family, physical
health, relationships, how you do your job, how you
serve your customers, how you manage people, and
personal time?

•If nothing changes, will the things you've gotten used to serve your needs over time?

If the answer to this second question is "no",
then you need to explore some ways to break out of
these traps.

Pendulum Change

The second way we process change is through
pendulum change. All of us have experienced this
process. Pendulum change occurs when something
happens that causes us to grab hold on the conscious
level and try hard to be different. This generally
follows a significant emotional event. A plant closure or a strike causes us to try hard to change, but
when things settle down, we fall back to the same
old behaviors. A drunk driving arrest causes us to
make an immediate pledge of sobriety, but in most
cases, as the experience dims in our memory, we may

again "have one for the road". After a major accident, we focus on safety, but we gradually and incrementally lose sight of the importance of safety as time goes by.

That significant emotional event, no matter what it is, motivates us to override who we are long enough to get what we want. Then we fall back to the same old behavior that created the problem in the first place.

Pendulum change is a temporary improvement; it doesn't last. It's like having company visit for a week. We get really involved in cleaning the house, getting everything in perfect order. Then when the company leaves, we breathe a sigh of relief and go back to our old procedures. Another example might be an audit at our work place. We get things cleaned up and everyone gets involved in their work until the audit team leaves and we can go back to normal behavior.

Inmates in prison will override who they are long enough to get out. They'll say all the right things, play all the right games, demonstrate all the right actions, but soon after their release, they begin to participate in activities that are destined to put them back in prison.

A few years ago, I had the unpleasant experience of needing heart surgery. I had a triple by-pass. Let me say, that gets your attention! For the first year or so, I was so disciplined in my eating that nothing passed my lips that had fat or cholesterol on the label. I was drinking milk that was so thin you could see through it! Then a year or so later, I found myself beginning to rationalize why I deserved a nice sirloin steak and a baked potato with the works.

It takes great discipline to make long-term change. It's so comfortable to fall back into old habits and behaviors. Pendulum change can be the beginning of long-term improvement, but it takes tremendous commitment and support. When you try hard to override all of your underlying habits, attitudes, beliefs and expectations, it takes tremendous will power for the new behaviors to become automated. Our tendency is to take the path of least resistance which leads us back to the familiar. Without new tools, change is very difficult at best. But, with new tools, change can be an exciting journey.

Some changes are hard to accept. In 1829 Martin Van Buren, then the governor of New York wrote this to the President: "The canal system of this country is being threatened by the spread of a new form of transportation known as 'railroads'. As you may well know, railroad carriages are pulled at the enormous speed of 15 miles per hour by engines, which, in addition to endangering life and limb of passengers, roar and snort their way through the countryside. The Almighty certainly never intended that people should travel at such breakneck speed."

Change by Exception

The third way we respond to the changes going on around us is called change by exception. We develop attitudes and beliefs that, over time, become our reality. When we are faced with anything that might conflict with our beliefs, we are able to rationalize the differences by labeling the person or situation an "exception". My own background would seem a barrier to many people, so if you believe a person like me can't change, you can at least accept me by labeling me an "exception".

For twenty years I've heard people say "You're an exception" when they become aware of my background. When I say, "People in prison can change; look at me," the response is generally "yes, but you're an exception." Why wasn't I an exception twenty-five years ago? I'm the same person; I've just changed the way I *think*. I can show you hundreds of men and women just like me who have changed their lives. They are contributing members of society. If we can provide new tools and at least minimal opportunities and a somewhat supportive environment, change is possible for large portions of the men and women locked up in our prison systems.

You can believe that certain groups are less able to work at certain jobs; then, when you see someone from that group who is excellent at the work you have excluded them from, you just label that person an exception in order to keep from changing your belief.

Change by exception can become a "cop out" for leadership. It allows organizations to neglect training even though there is evidence that training is a valuable asset to the people in the organization. "He's an exception." "Most people don't benefit from training!" "She's an exception; most women couldn't perform that kind of work!" "He's an exception; most young people aren't responsible." "She's an exception; most people her age couldn't take care of themselves."

At one time the railroads were a male-dominated work environment. Then a woman became an engineer. She was labeled an "exception". Then another woman became an engineer; another exception. Then another, and another, and gradually the exception became the norm. It seems we as society are threatened by people who do better than we think they should. Instead, we should work to create an environment where exceptions can flourish; a place where individuals can use their talents and creativity and be rewarded for becoming an exception. This is a nice vision for all of us to pursue.

Paradigm Change

Paradigm change has become the 1990's corporate buzzword. Training literature abounds with phrases wrapped around the word "paradigm". Using the definition of the 90's, a paradigm is a frame of reference. Stephen Covey, author of "Seven Habits of Highly Effective People," uses the analogy of a map in our minds; a road map that we follow as we journey through life. A map that is outdated, or a map of Chicago if you are in Seattle, would be of little use.

Change is gradual and takes time. A paradigm shift speeds up the process. Today we need to constantly ask ourselves why we do what we do, and whether it adds value to the end result we are trying to accomplish. We need to provide a new framework for change. Abraham Maslow has a great quote: "If the only tool you have is a hammer, then you view every problem as a nail." We need to offer new tools and an environment where change can take place.

The key to change is the application of new concepts and techniques. You start by beginning to move forward. The book, "Blundering to Glory" by Owen Connelly, suggests that Napoleon may not have been that great as a general, but he kept moving and was in the right place at the right time. He blundered to glory. If you want to make change happen, you need to get moving. You don't lose weight by chance, you do it by changing your eating habits and by increasing your exercise routine. You don't improve quality by chance, you do it by changing to a culture that expects quality. This takes follow-through and commitment. Change is possible, but it's a do-it-yourself project. We need to let go of the past and set forth on this exciting journey called "change".

3. Barriers To Change

What holds us back and keeps us "stuck" are the major barriers to change. I want to discuss how these barriers develop. There are always other factors, but these are the barriers that become major obstacles to long-term improvement. When you consider the concepts covered here, I'd like you to look at them both personally and professionally.

The first, and probably the most difficult barrier to overcome, is our pre-conditioned, cultural beliefs. If you change your beliefs, you change your performance.

The second barrier to change is our habits and outdated skills. We get habituated in our behaviors and our habits become obstacles to change.

The third is our attitudes. We develop attitudes that control how we act and how we participate in life.

The fourth is our expectations. Expectations create comfort zones that keep us stuck. You don't get what you *want* in life, you get what you expect. Now let's go back and explore each of the four in more detail.

Pre-conditioned Cultural Beliefs

First, as you all know, we don't come into this world with a pre-determined set of beliefs. But, as we interact with our world, we gradually develop our truth about who we are and what we can and cannot do. We develop truths about who has power and how the world works. The beliefs then begin to control what we do and how we do it on a daily basis. When I talk about beliefs, I'm not referring to our religious beliefs, but rather the pre-conditioning that comes from our environments. Let's look at some examples.

There was a time in history when people operated and made decisions based on the belief that the earth was flat. At that time, ships would sail out just so far and then sailors would chicken out, turn around and head back to shore. Now, if you believe the world is flat and that it's possible to fall off the edge, heading back to shore is not chickening out; it's good common sense!

Every time we try to implement change we go up against this same challenge. This is true both personally and organizationally. I can look back at my own life and see all of the beliefs that I'd picked up and how they trapped me. Until I shifted my beliefs, I was swimming against the current, trying hard but making minimal progress. If we examine all of the beliefs that impact how we live our lives, we find that most of our beliefs have been formed by accepting opinions and truths from other people who are projecting their reality of the world as if it were universal truth. Imagine forming your reality of how to succeed in life behind the walls of a maximum security prison! It may serve your needs to learn this reality in prison, but it will put you in conflict with society once you're outside the walls. The globalization of the world economy, new technology, and a changing marketplace has made many of our past practices obsolete. Age, sex, race, religion, education, and national origin are all areas where our pre-conditioned cultural beliefs become barriers to change.

However, we can speed up the process of change when we free ourselves from past conditioning. When I realized that most of the challenges I faced were self-imposed, it created a major paradigm shift in how I approached life. It felt like someone had released the anchor that had kept me stuck and suddenly I was flowing *with* the current. To just change the way you look at challenges, seeing the possibility of solutions, instead of being mired down in problems, can be an eye-opening experience. What if we could solve this challenge? What if we could work together in harmony? What if they followed through? What if...?

As individuals and as groups, we need to examine our beliefs by first identifying what they are. This is not an easy thing to do. It takes time and serious self-examination. But it is an extremely worthwhile thing to do. Once we identify our beliefs, we need to ask ourselves where they came from. Knowing the source of our beliefs can help us establish their relevance to our lives. It is amazing how many beliefs we carry around which, when exposed to new light, suddenly strike us as glaringly absurd.

Having increased our awareness about our beliefs, we can continue the process of asking questions.

- Is this belief still relevant in today's world?
- Are my beliefs biased?
- Do my beliefs foster cooperation and involvement?

If not, then the first step to making lasting change is to restructure the beliefs.

> **If you change your belief, you
> change your performance.**
> **GG**

It would be ridiculous in today's world to try to sell people on the belief that the earth is flat. We would want to lock that person away! But we develop flat worlds in our minds, limiting beliefs, that control our behavior just as much as they did before the discovery that the earth was round. We have flat world beliefs about how smart we are, how creative we are, what we can and can't do based on our past, our race, our age, or because "they" won't listen. To truly become aware that you can make a difference, that you have the power to change and become a positive force in your company or your community, is a powerful motivator. For some people, this awareness comes with the swiftness of light; a sudden illumination, a break-through that transcends time, a paradigm shift. For others, it is a gradual change, an accumulation of experiences, an increase in knowledge and self-confidence that opens up new vistas as the past fades into nothingness. The illumination or paradigm shift comes from self-referral, a sudden realization of who one really is. The slow, gradual change results from object referral; confirmation from other people or an external reference point.

A paradigm shift causes a transformation. It's a conscious realization that we have the internal power to control our life. It frees us from past conditioning; we accept ourselves as masters of our lives.

They train huge elephants by attaching one end of a logging chain to the elephant's leg and the other end to the trunk of a large tree or a strong cement post. The elephant fights the chain, lunging against the controlling chain to no avail. Gradually, the elephant accepts that its movement is limited to a certain radius. The trainer then reduces the size of the chain until finally the elephant can be controlled by a rope the size of your little finger. Many of us have gradually limited ourselves through our experiences and our conditioning to only try those things that are safe, until finally we are like the elephant, controlled by our internal image of reality. A paradigm shift is created by the realization that you can break the chains that hold you back.

Pre-conditioned beliefs, added to the fact that we may have tried something in the past and failed, are major obstacles to change. An honest assessment of where we are, our current reality, and what beliefs are keeping us stuck, is essential. The concept of G.I./G.O. (garbage in/garbage out) used in computer technology is also a truism in life. Working harder won't achieve our goals if we're working from the wrong paradigm. We need to change the way our computers, our brains, are programmed if we want different results in our lives.

A few key questions to ask yourself:
•What do I believe about my ability to change?
•How do I feel about my own power to impact my work group?
•What beliefs do I hold that may be a product of misinformation?

In my own life, I accumulated a ton of garbage that kept me in a perpetual rut for thirty-seven years. I allowed other people to predict my future. I accepted a picture of reality that would have kept me in prisons for the rest of my life. I was blessed to have been exposed to new information that shifted my perceptions of myself and of the world around me. But, there are many people like myself who are operating from a belief system that keeps them in prison. It may not be a prison of bars and steel, but rather a prison in their mind that is stronger and more difficult to overcome than bars and steel. The first part of an escape plot is to examine beliefs and take back your own power. Change is an inside job; but we need new tools.

Habits

The second major barrier to change is our habits. We become habituated as human beings. The things we do on a daily basis become automated. We gradually lose conscious awareness of the behavior. The definition of insanity is continuing to do the same things and expecting different results.

The next time you are home for a family dinner sit in a different chair than you normally sit in. You will throw the whole family off. "That's my chair!" We sit in the same chairs, we go through the same preparation as we start our day. This is fine until something changes or until we become bored with life. In companies, people get into a routine; they go through the same motions, talk to the same people, listen to the same people, walk the same routes, sit at the same tables, and then someone comes in and tries to implement change, and it puts everyone in an uproar!

I taught my oldest daughter, Tami, how to drive in a stick shift automobile. I'd take her to the country where there was no traffic and put her behind the wheel. Then I would give her the instructions. "Put your foot on the clutch and shift into low gear.

Now let your foot off the clutch." She'd drop the clutch, and I'd give her feedback. "A little slower, Tami." She'd get the car moving in low gear. I'd say, "Okay now put your foot on the clutch and shift into second." She'd drop the clutch and kill the motor. I'd tell her, "Tami, you're going to tear the transmission out. Let the clutch out slowly." The only reason I had for telling her she'd tear the transmission out is that someone told me that! I don't have the foggiest idea whether it would tear the transmission out! Hell, I don't even know if they still have transmissions! What do you think Tami might tell her children? "Don't drop the clutch or you'll tear the transmission out!" If someone questions her wisdom she'll probably say, "My dad told me so!" How many times have you heard that response? "Joe said, and he's been there thirty years."

Within a couple of months, Tami was able to drive down the street 45 miles per hour in a 30-mile per hour zone. She was driving with one hand on the wheel, chewing gum, changing channels on the radio, talking to a friend in the passenger's seat, looking out both windows for boys and the rear view mirror for the police, all at the same time! How could she do that? The skills and habits became automated. The only time she messed up was when she tried to drive a car with an automatic transmission. She'd come up to a stop sign and throw you into the windshield. If you said, "Tami, stop slamming on the brakes like that!" her response was, "I thought it was the clutch!"

There is nothing wrong with skills and habits as long as no one changes the machinery on you, or the competition doesn't improve, or the world doesn't change. We face the same challenge if our skills and habits are outdated, or if we pick up skills and habits from someone who is not an authority in the subject matter. The habit of waiting for someone to tell you what to do kills creativity. But, if the culture reinforces this type of management it becomes very difficult to change.

Ask yourself these questions:

•What habits have we developed in our work environment, that may no longer be relevant?

•What skills have become obsolete?

•What personal habits have I developed that keep me stuck?

The habits and skills that you develop in a prison environment become obstacles to success on the streets. The habits and skills that worked in the years of a national economy become obstacles to success in a global world. Many habits and skills serve us well. But when circumstances change, we may need new ones to adapt to and succeed in the change.

Attitudes

The third barrier to change is attitudes. We develop attitudes that affect how we deal with people and how we approach our lives and our world. The best way I've found to explain an attitude is to look at it in aeronautical terms. A pilot has a panel of instruments that provides feedback on the plane's operations. One instrument gives the attitude of the plane. The attitude is determined by how the wing span leans in relation to a fixed point on the horizon. If you want to change the attitude, you change the way the wings tilt. For you and I, our attitude is determined by how we lean on a subconscious level. If we lean toward certain people, foods, or activities, we are said to have a positive attitude about that particular person or thing. If we lean away and avoid something, we are said to have a negative attitude. However, we don't set out to get an attitude about something. We don't do it consciously or deliberately. Attitudes are developed through knowledge or experiences with emotional impact. Many times we develop attitudes about things we have never experienced. We develop attitudes about places we've never visited, people we've never met and foods we've never tasted.

I was speaking to a group of little league football players a few years ago. I had about 400 young men from 9 to 12 years old and all of their parents and coaches. The youngsters were in the front rows and I was talking to them about attitudes that make a good team player. I wanted them to understand how their attitudes were developed so I asked them a question: "How many of you don't like liver and onions?" Most of the young people raised their hands. There was a young man about 10 years old in the front row who raised his hand. I asked him, "Son, how many times have you eaten liver and onions?" His response brought a burst of laughter from the audience as he said, "I've never eaten it." "Then how do you know you don't like it?", I asked. "My brothers and sisters don't like it. Nobody in my family likes liver and onions." This young man will go through his entire life with that attitude. If his mom or dad forced him to eat liver and onions he'd probably get sick.

Imagine all of the attitudes we develop in similar ways. Having an attitude about liver and onions will have little impact on our lives, but other attitudes developed in the same way can play a major role in how we live our lives. If we have an awareness of how our attitudes are formed, then we can begin to change or modify the attitudes that are affecting our physical or mental health, our financial well-being, our performance on our jobs, and even our relationships.

I can remember when I had a negative attitude about dancing. I didn't dance. I'd never tried to dance; I just had a negative attitude about it. My wife had a positive attitude about dancing; she really enjoyed it. We would go out to an evening event where dancing was a part of the entertainment and I would automatically find a place to sit in the middle of a booth that made it very difficult to get out. My wife would ask, "Do you want to dance?"

and my response would be, "I'd like to, but I can't get out", or "Let's wait till there's a slow one." If I thought there was going to be a slow dance, I'd go to the men's room. These actions were creative avoidance techniques triggered by my attitude about dancing. I've found some people will overcome their negative attitude about dancing with a few shots of Jack Daniels. Unfortunately, the next morning they can't remember whether they danced or sang. We develop attitudes about certain types of people, attitudes about cooperation, attitudes about change and these attitudes keep us stuck in the same old rut.

The culture in an industrial plant plays a major role in the attitude concerning union and management relations, communication, teamwork, cooperation and how the customer is viewed. We also develop attitudes about whole groups of people. I've talked to managers who have an attitude about unions and when I ask which one they're referring to, their response is, "All of them!" But, like everything else, there's good and bad. Union people will have the same negative attitudes about management. No, there is good and bad in most everything and everyone. Our attitude determines whether we develop healthy or toxic relationships.

Expectations and Comfort Zones

We are born into this world with a blank canvas in our mind. It is suggested that we are predisposed toward certain strengths or weaknesses based on our genetic code, but in terms of habits, attitudes, beliefs, and expectations, the canvas is clean. We then begin to put brush strokes on the canvas through our experiences and information that we pick up from the world around us. We gradually paint a picture in our brain of who we are; this picture is referred to as a self-image or a self-concept. Based on this picture, we develop a corresponding comfort zone. The comfort zone is where we fit. It's our rut. It's neither good nor bad; it just is. The only time the comfort zone becomes a challenge is when we try to change. Comfort zones can be very narrow, like an Archie Bunker, where only people like ourselves are okay. We develop comfort zones socially and environmentally. Comfort zones can also keep us protected. It's essential that we know when we face danger. A comfort zone that's too wide can get us into serious trouble. I always felt my daughter's comfort zone was too wide. She would go places that caused me to be under extreme stress.

The self-image is our expectation and it's our truth. As long as we stay consistent, we're all right. But when we try to change, we get feedback that tells us we don't belong. The key is to understand comfort zones and know how to expand in areas that are appropriate.

This concept was brought to my awareness with emotional impact a few years ago. I'd been out of prison for a number of years and was feeling good about my life. I was presenting seminars on change to prison staff, inmates, military groups and government agencies. I'd been able to overcome the comfort zone challenges and had even taught workshops at the FBI Academy in Quanico, Virginia. My background was an open book. I'd never tried to hide the fact that I'd been in prison for seventeen years. Prison officials, law enforcement leaders, agency heads and business groups had accepted me for who I had become: an honest, contributing member of society. Then I came face to face with the fact that some people develop attitudes about whole groups of people and you can allow these attitudes to control how you live your life.

I'd conducted a number of workshops for military corrections at the FBI Academy. Jim Murphy, a member of the United States Marshal's Service, participated in a couple of these workshops and we became friends. He called me one day from his office in Washington, D.C. and asked if I'd be interested in presenting a four-hour seminar on change to a group of marshals who were going through a career transition. The training was to take place at the Federal Law Enforcement Training Facility in Glenco, Georgia. It sounded interesting and gave me an opportunity to break another barrier. A guy with my background working with the United States Marshals would be a real demonstration of what can happen if you change and stay focused. I told Jim I'd be happy to be involved.

I flew to Atlanta and then took a small commuter plan to Glenco. Glenco is a former military installation where a number of law enforcement agencies conducted a wide range of training activities. When I arrived, I checked into one of the few motels. My presentation wasn't until the next morning, but Jim Murphy had recommended that I listen to the speaker who would be speaking prior to me. He told me that the guy's presentation style was great and he was speaking on hostage negotiations. You never know when you might want to take a hostage so the subject matter was interesting. I dressed in a suit and tie (you can't tell the good guys from the bad guys if they're dressed in a suit and tie). I took a shuttle to the facility, checked in, and got directions to the training room. There were about fifty marshals in the audience and the speaker was using an overhead projector to illustrate a point on negotiations. I found an empty chair in the back of the room and took out a note pad. The speaker had a nice delivery and kept the audience involved with questions and a nice blend of humor.

When the speaker released us for a break, people were milling around, getting coffee, and discussing the presentation. I was leaning against a wall, away from the group. (It's always a comfort zone challenge for me to mingle with a group of strangers. It's especially difficult if the group is law enforcement people who don't know me.) A couple of marshals were walking by and I overhead one of them say, "You know what I heard? They told me they've got some dirt bag ex-con coming in here to speak to us!" My first thought was, "I wonder why they would do that?" Then it hit me, "Hell, he's talking about me!" My next thought was, "I wonder if there's a plane going out of here tonight? Hell, I don't need this!" But, I checked myself and thought about how his attitude was developed. It was based on all negative experiences and it's also a protective mechanism. I really couldn't fault him for his attitude, but I also chose not to let his attitude affect the way I live my life.

I went back to my room and reviewed my presentation and thought about the great opportunity I had to help this group see a different picture of an ex-con. I visualized a successful presentation and saw the marshals as friends. The next morning when I was introduced as the speaker, I was ready. It was one of my best presentations and, as a result, I have many friends in the Marshal's Service. But, there was a time when I would have let that one person's attitude control my life. Back then I was out of my comfort zone speaking to the marshals. Gradually and incrementally, though, I've expanded my comfort zone to the point where it doesn't impact me at all.

How many times do we let the negative attitudes of a few people affect our whole plant? We may not be able to change other people's attitudes, but we can make a choice not to let them impact how we live our lives.

In summary, if we want to create a change in our lives, we need to identify the beliefs, habits, and attitudes that are keeping us stuck. Then, we can *choose* new beliefs and attitudes that will support the changes we want to make. As a result of the new beliefs and attitudes, our habits change almost automatically. Even though we may initially be out of our comfort zone, gradually and incrementally our comfort zone will expand to include the new beliefs and attitudes and our new habits will become normal, accepted behavior.

Man cannot discover new oceans unless he has the courage to lose sight of the shore.
                    Andre Gide/Nobel Prize Winner

4. The Organizational Experience

My first introduction to industrial plants resulted from a chance meeting with a member of the United Auto Workers (U.A.W.). I'd been invited to speak at a spiritual retreat being held at the Asylamar Conference Center in Northern California. Asylamar is a beautiful serene setting with rustic buildings scattered among evergreens and flowering shrubs. The walking trails lead down to the sandy beaches of the Pacific Ocean, allowing spiritual seekers an opportunity to commune with their God while they experience the mighty power of the ocean. It's an ideal location to escape the frantic pace of life, but not a place that you'd associate with the U.A.W. and industrial plants!

The morning after my presentation, I was out enjoying Asylamar's beauty. I was walking along one of the paths that led down to the water. My thoughts were off somewhere in space, when I was brought back to earth by a large man with white hair and a flowing mustache. He was sitting on a rock ledge that ran along the path. "I really enjoyed your presentation last night." His remark caused me to stop and reply, "Thanks, I thought the group was great." I vaguely remembered the guy as one of the "huggers." After my talk it seemed like everyone wanted to hug me! I'm talking women *and* men! I wasn't a hugger in those days, and it's still out of my comfort zone to have some big ol' dude come up and throw his arms around me.

The guy continued, "I'm Paul Bluto with the U.A.W. I'd like to have you speak to a group of our shop stewards sometime." I thought, "What the hell is a shop steward?" but I responded, "Sure, I'd like to do that."

He asked for my business card. Business cards had just recently become a part of my life. After we exchanged cards, I continued down the path to the beach. The vast expanse of the Pacific Ocean put things in perspective for me. The awesome power of nature brings renewal to the soul. Paul Bluto and the U.A.W. were worlds away as I looked out over the soft swells of the Pacific and thought about how far I'd come from the cellblocks of Walla Walla.

Six months later, Paul, who turned out to be the Education Director for Region Six of the U.A.W., called my office. He wanted me to make a presentation to a group of shop stewards for his region. The group was going to be in Pellston, Michigan for some training and Paul wanted me to be part of the program. I remembered our conversation at Asylamar and instructed my office to see if we could work it out. I still didn't know what a shop steward did, but I figured I could learn by the time I reached Pellston.

My schedule had me in Fairbanks, Alaska the day before Paul wanted me in Michigan and there were no airline flights that would get me to Michigan in time for the session. Katie, my assistant, informed Paul that I wouldn't be able to accommodate him because of airline schedules. Paul's response was "Can you get him to Los Angeles by midnight? We're chartering planes and flying our people to Black Lake. If he can hook up with us at L.A.X., we'll get him the rest of the way!" Katie checked schedules and got me on a flight from Fairbanks to Los Angeles. I arrived at L.A.X. about eleven o'clock in the evening and met Paul. There was a crowd milling around and a couple of people with clipboards checking names and assigning seats. Paul introduced me to some of the union leaders and then I tried to fade into the background and escape the questions and interaction that was still out of my comfort zone. This was a different group of people than I'd found at most conferences. There were no suits or ties, and no apparent hierarchy (although I found later that the hierarchy did exist). Most of the men and women were dressed in jeans and wore union jackets that proclaimed "United Auto Workers". There were lots of baseball caps loaded with union pins. The greetings included a lot of "How you doin', Brother?" or "What's goin' on, Sister?" The unions were big on brotherhood and sisterhood in meetings and conferences, but I've since discovered that this doesn't always carry over to the plant floor.

When everyone was assembled, we boarded two chartered 737's and headed for Pellston, Michigan, a small town (with an airport that has a very short runway) about twenty miles from Black Lake and the U.A.W.'s National Training Center.

We arrived at Pellston about 8:00 the next morning and were met by busses from the Training Center. The group was much more subdued after flying all night, especially those who had enjoyed the company of Jack Daniels. When we got to the Training Center, our rooms were still occupied by a group just finishing a training program and there was no place for our people to rest after the long flight from Los Angeles. Paul Bluto managed to get a room cleaned and ready for me. (Speakers seem to get a little extra attention at workshops and conferences which makes it nice, especially if you're tired and want some privacy.)

I showered and changed clothes. My presentation wasn't until after dinner so I went out to see what the U.A.W. Training Center looked like. Black Lake lies in a beautiful part of Michigan. The grounds are covered with trees and other greenery. The training facilities compare with some of the best in the country. I later discovered why you might see a union steward or committee person carrying a few extra pounds. The food is one of the many talked-about features at Black Lake. The quality and preparation is outstanding and the quantity almost forces you to give up dieting for the duration of your stay.

As I strolled through the grounds, as always, I thought back to where I'd come from; cellblocks and the joint mess hall. It seemed a lifetime ago. To look back at that part of my life through the eyes of a person who is honest and who has experienced a total shift in beliefs, habits, attitudes and values is like looking at another person. Who was that guy? How could a person get trapped in a lifestyle of dishonesty, prisons and convicts? I'm still the same person; I just think differently. The awareness and the knowing frees you from the past.

As I reflected on my life, I turned my thoughts to the evening's presentation. I'd done some research on the union/management situation since I agreed to participate at Black Lake. There seemed to be a history of conflict and confrontation. There was a strong sense of "us" against "them". It seemed that the whole structure of collective bargaining reinforced this belief. It was almost as if there were two separate sets of rules. The union could do almost anything against management and would be supported by the union brothers and sisters. Management could undermine the union, institute unfair practices, or make blatant decisions concerning distribution of moneys and was supported by the management hierarchy. The relationships were tenuous at best, one act away from a grievance, lawsuit, or at worst, a strike. This reminded me very much of prison. Many of the same conditions and practices make up the culture of a joint. A sad commentary, but that's the way it looked from my vantage point.

I had decided on my approach to the evening presentation. I intended to give them an overview of the change process, then a review of the major barriers to long-term change, and what can happen when there is a paradigm shift. My background and my journey through negative conditioning would be my platform. What gives power to a presentation are examples that make participants think, "Damn! He's talking about me," or "He's been reading our mail."

That night, after one of the famous Black Lake dinners, the 300 or so union members were feeling more like a good sleep than listening to a speaker. I was thinking that Paul Bluto had probably ended any chance of me ever being invited to another union workshop. There's a specific format that union meetings follow: a recognition of the U.S. flag, a formal request for God's blessing and a call for union solidarity. I've never seen a group that has a stronger sense of what being an American is all about than the U.A.W.

There were six or seven people at the head table with me when the introductions began; the Regional Director, a couple of people from Solidarity House in Detroit, and one or two additional members who apparently had some special status. That night I learned another thing about union leaders: they can give a speech. So as each person at the head table was introduced, a short political call-to-arms followed. I was getting very concerned about my presentation. "By the time they get to me the whole damn group will be asleep," I thought. Finally the last person at the head table had been given his accolades and it was time to introduce the featured speaker. They had a short bio that didn't really say much about me. I didn't have a best seller on unions or management, no prestigious position or title, and no claim to fame except that I came highly recommended by Brother Paul Bluto.

There were a few kind souls who put their hands together as I came to the microphone, more out of pity than anything else. When I started my presentation, there was very little response from the 300 tired, maxed-out union brothers and sisters.

They'd flown all night, hadn't slept, and after a fine meal and a couple of glasses of wine, they were tired. I could sense an uneasiness at the head table. They weren't sure how this was going to play out. What if the speaker bombed? Would it affect their status? How can we shorten this talk? I could feel the questions; they didn't have to be spoken.

There's a point in a talk when you know the group is ready. If you bring certain points in too soon they won't hear. I've been gifted with a mastery of timing. I began by laying out my background. "I left home at an early age and grew up on the streets. As a result of 'poor management' I wound up as a consumer of correctional services. I've done seventeen years in maximum security prisons. I've been shot, stabbed, escaped from maximum security prisons and, at one time in my life, I did a year on bread and water." As I spoke, I could feel the change in the room. People were sitting up in their chairs. You could hear the question, "What did he say?" There was a shift in energy as I continued, "Prisons create cultures that reinforce the 'us' versus 'them' attitude. It's the convict against 'The Man'. There are different rules for different groups. I've not been involved in the union/management world very long, but there seems to be some very similar conditions in your world."

My presentation was scheduled for one hour, but at the end of the hour they asked me to continue. I spoke for two solid hours and closed with a powerful poem entitled, "The Cold Within". The standing ovation lasted for several minutes. This was one of the highlights of my career. The United Auto Workers became my friends and they have been my advocates in many industrial plants. As a result of my experience at Black Lake, I have become much more familiar with unions and collective bargaining.

To make changes in an industrial plant from an autocratic structure that is hierarchical, to an empowered organization where you involve the hearts and minds of the employees is one of this country's greatest challenges. Since the beginning of the global economy and the invasion of competitors from Japan to Germany, we have struggled with how to compete more effectively in the global arena. William Edwards Deming and other experts have long espoused harnessing the creative genius of employees. The theory suggests that the person doing the work may well be the one best qualified to find ways to improve quality and productivity. We sent massive groups of experts to Japan to discover what they were doing that made them so effective. The message came back that they had self-government, that the people doing the work were involved. They had implemented Deming's and Juran's theories that had been ignored by a society that had a monopoly on the market place. Words began to creep into our vernacular like Kaizan (continuous improvement) and just-in-time inventory.

At the plant level, workers had never before been invited to the party. They had been hired from the neck down and now they were being asked to think! Managers were measured on output, getting things done, not on how they treated employees. Supervisors, mid-managers and upper management were accustomed to giving orders, not to seeking input from their subordinates. There was little trust between the labor force and management. Rewards were on short-term achievements. "How will it show up on the bottom line?" was the manager's major concern, while the union leaders were asking, "Will it get me re-elected?".

I became involved with union/management just as the new paradigm was unfolding. The similarities between my prison experiences of the seventies, and the frenzy to incorporate Japanese management theories and to humanize our industrial plants in the Eighties were startling. To take a concept titled "self government" and try to implement it in one of the most volatile, dangerous prisons in the country seems insane at best, and a blatant disregard for human lives at worst. I would lean toward the first, because I'm convinced that those making the decisions were decent people. But, to expect an industrial plant that has operated for fifty years as a hierarchical organization to become an organization where everyone is valued and listened to, and where there is trust between union and management is fantasy at best and corporate suicide at worst.

However, the possibility of making these kinds of changes in an industrial plant, with intense pre-planning, a true commitment from both union and top level management, and a willingness to think long-term, have begun to have some profound results. A dramatic increase in quality, productivity and innovative solutions that flow from the rank and file, give testimony to this philosophy. We have certainly taken many of the principles from Deming, Juran and others and incorporated them into an American work force. We have taken the strengths from the plants in Japan and modified them so they fit in our culture. It is an American solution.

Another common denominator between correctional systems and industry in the 1980's was money. There was an abundance of resources available to throw at the problem. In the Seventies, hundreds of state, federal and private players in the correctional game flew first class to resorts for two to five day conferences on prison reform. Speakers abounded.

This became one of my first platforms. I found myself being flown to heretofore unheard of locations
to speak about the life of a convict behind bars and
now on release. This was all on the federal dollar.
Keynote speakers with long impressive vitaes were
paid handsome honorariums to espouse the latest
theory on rehabilitation. Long hair, beards and an
assortment of garish garb brought a sense of status
to the presenter. Uncle Sam had deep pockets then
and the pockets were being picked by an uncontrolled parade of self-proclaimed experts. The victims of this lavishly funded debacle were the inmates caught up in prisons across the United States
and the taxpayers who were paying for it.

The Eighties saw the same uncontrolled spending in the industrial plants across the United States.
Planeloads of union and management people were
flown across the Pacific to visit the industrial plants
in Japan. Conventions and conferences were held
off-site at locations in Florida, Arizona, and Nevada.
Keynote speakers with impressive academic creden-
tials and books on the best seller list were flown in
to tell the group how ineffective and outdated they
were, and how terribly efficient and productive our
competitors had become. They included a good bit
of humor and suggested that if the group would only
pay attention to the speaker's latest book, abundance
and prosperity were at arm's reach. They generally
received a standing ovation for beating the audience
up, sold a large number of books and left with hono-

rariums of at least five figures. Those who suffered from this tremendous investment of resources were the dedicated employees struggling to keep their plant functional during this search for a magic formula. We have finally begun to look inside, to the people. This is where the answers will eventually be found.

The NUMMI Experiment

Hamtramck was designed as the flagship for General Motors. It was equipped with the ultimate in technology and automation, a huge sprawling industrial complex located in the suburbs of Detroit, Michigan.

When I first became involved with Hamtramck, they were still in the early stages of establishing how the plant was to operate. There were approximately 6,000 employees spread across three shifts. The plant assembled the top of the line automobiles produced by General Motors; the Cadillac, the Riviera, and the newly designed sporty Allante. This was the early Eighties and the reality of global competition had not yet impacted the U.A.W. and General Motors. In spite of a declining market share and an influx of foreign automobiles, General Motors seemed to be immune. The attitude that "this too will pass", had become imbedded in the corporate culture. There were many short-term efforts to bring about meaningful change. It was as though there was an answer somewhere out there, waiting to be discovered. The search became a disconnected series of forays by union and management to find the magic pill that could change their culture and bring back the good old days.

Management and union leaders became infatuated with the industrial plants in Japan. Planeloads of U.A.W. and General Motors leaders invaded Toyota and Nissan, looking for the answer. They returned to their plants with new terms like Kaizan, "fix the problem/not the blame", and "just-in-time inventory"; only to find that the culture in the U.S. did not readily accept these new ideas.

General Motors, Toyota, and the U.A.W. formed a joint venture to develop an assembly plant that would incorporate the best practices of both Toyota and General Motors. This new venture was called New United Motors Manufacturing, Inc., more commonly referred to as NUMMI. The plant was located in Fremont, California, a small community across the Bay Bridge from San Francisco. The experiment with new practices and new work rules became an overwhelming success. NUMMI began to attract visitors like an industrial version of Disneyland. It was perceived in industrial circles as the panacea. The U.A.W. leaders at NUMMI became heroes and were sought-after speakers at conferences and conventions. Labor relations and management personnel alike were elevated to guru status.

When I first became involved in the NUMMI experience, I was amazed at the kind of attention it was generating as a model for U.S. industrial plants. However, there were so many features that were unique to NUMMI. The most obvious was the fact that the existing Fremont plant had been closed for some time. The realities of losing jobs and income had already been experienced by the employees and the community. A new labor agreement had been established prior to hiring people for the NUMMI plant. Applicants were told, "This is how we are managing the plant. Do you want to work under this agreement?" It offered an opportunity for industrial workers to make a choice prior to accepting a job. Japanese management, General Motors' management, and U.A.W. members were involved from the start. They also had the luxury of starting slow and working out the bugs prior to full-scale production. Being viewed as an industry leader undoubtedly was a powerful, though intangible, motivator. When newspapers, trade journals and visitors from all over the world reinforce your success, it certainly contributes to your positive image.

These unique features at NUMMI set it apart from the majority of industrial plants who are trying to "fix their bicycles while they ride them." To implement change in a corporate culture that has developed over 50 years of confrontation and conflict is much more challenging, and to do this while you continue to meet production schedules is next to impossible.

The steering committee from Hamtramck (the union/management leadership) spent a week at NUMMI to evaluate this industrial phenomenon. Because of the backlog of visitors at NUMMI, the amount of time the group from Hamtramck could spend in the plant was limited. The large block of time they spent waiting presented quite a challenge. "How do we keep the people engaged in some meaningful activity? Hell, let's train them." Training, regardless of its value, is a great time-filler! This need opened a window of opportunity and I became the filler. Out of this opportunity, my association with Hamtramck began. Both the union and the management recognized the need to bring my message on change to the employees at Hamtramck.

During our time at NUMMI, we reached an agreement to bring *A Framework for Change* training process into the Hamtramck assembly plant. *A Framework for Change* addresses the cultural issues of an organization. The culture is made up of pre-conditioned beliefs, habits, attitudes, comfort zones, and the subtle group dynamics that are hard to measure but have a dramatic impact on the bottom line. The first phase would be for me to deliver a live presentation to all 6,000 employees. This was to be done over a week's time, in 12 groups of 500; two sessions each day for 6 days, 1,000 people per day. This would include all shifts of both hourly and salaried employees.

The experience at Hamtramck was one of the most challenging I'd undertaken. There was great support from the leadership of both union and management, but I doubt that either side expected anything to change. In fact, one of the key management people told me, "Gordy, we never follow through on anything. You've got to stay on us or nothing will happen." His comment proved to be true.

The live presentations were held in the final assembly area of the plant. Hamtramck is a huge complex, covering acres of land. The final assembly area was half the size of a football field. Long rows of metal folding chairs were arranged across the cement floor. Box-like speakers, a microphone, and an overhead projector were set up for my use. The acoustics caused my voice to have a metallic hollow sound as it bounced off the gray walls. It reminded me of the old cellblocks that had been my home for so many years.

The sessions were mandatory for all employees which, even under ideal circumstances, presents a challenge, but in the setting at Hamtramck it put me in a no-win situation. It was early in my career, and I wasn't secure enough to object to the conditions. I was also unaware that the hourly employees were working without a contract and negotiations were underway. I later realized that I was seen as a ploy by management to soften the employees for negotiations. I thought they just didn't *like* me.

When the groups began to assemble, they filled the back rows first, then began to move chairs off to the side, or even further back, leaving a huge, empty space between myself and the participants. Arms were folded with a "let's get this damn thing over with" attitude. The week seemed like a lifetime. I was exhausted at the end of each day. Working with inmates seemed like a joyous experience compared to the Hamtramck work force. I was unfamiliar with the idea of a toxic culture. But if a culture can become toxic, this was a prime example.

No one sets out to create this type of culture; it develops over time. One on one, people all want the same thing: to be treated with respect, listened to, involved, and fairly compensated. Yet, as a group, they became dysfunctional. The culture drives the performance of an organization. Any attempt to implement meaningful change without engaging the hearts and minds of employees is like swimming against a strong current. It's like putting wax on a dirty car. It doesn't work.

Hamtramck was a great learning experience. I continued to work with the plant for the next year. During that time, they were in the throes of change. At times, it seemed to me there was total chaos. No one appeared to be in charge. The midnight shift was like yard-out in the joint; employees engaged in card games, reading newspapers, or just hanging out. My concern was for the employees. I thought to myself, "How can they survive? This won't work long-term."

This apparent madness was one of the early attempts to engage the employees, or in today's technology, to empower people. But, to make the transition from an autocratic, hierarchical organization to an empowered organization, there needs to be a plan, some structure, and a bridge between these two opposing philosophies.

I'd experienced something like this before. In the late Sixties and early Seventies there was a misguided attempt to instill "self government" in a maximum security prison. Without planning, no structure, no involvement by prison guards (the line staff), the experiment resulted in anarchy. The same challenge exists in cultures that have gradually and incrementally developed an autocratic style of management. When you get used to someone giving orders, or telling you what to do and this doesn't happen, you just sit down and wait for someone to tell you. If someone asks, "Why didn't you do the job?" The response will be, "No one told me what to do." If you are a middle manager or a supervisor, and your people start to think and take control, your reason for existence is threatened. This is the paradox that many organizations face.

I've watched the interaction between union and management over the past sixteen or seventeen years. The words have changed from quality circles to employee involvement, from employee involvement to partnerships and from partnerships to self-directed teams and empowerment, but the underlying paradigm remains the same. In most organizations, the mentality is still "us" versus "them"; union against management and vice versa. Membership in unions has steadily declined over the past two decades. It is nearly impossible to work efficiently toward a common vision as long as management holds onto the belief that unions are obstacles to productivity and that the real answer is to decertify (get rid of) them. The union's belief that management will screw them if they don't fight for every advantage just creates a self-fulfilling prophecy. Throw in the politics of the union, and the struggle for power and position by management, and you have a structure that is a formidable challenge to change, to say the least. Fairness, equitable sharing of profits, the creative involvement of employees, the recognition that the world is becoming smaller and that competition demands change, is lost in the battle as both sides fight to keep what they've worked so long to achieve. When huge bonuses are paid to executives while employees are asked for more production as the company continues losing money, trust in management is eroded and reinforces the belief that there's no real concern for the employee's future.

Individuals working for their own best interests are

not good for the whole country. American management and labor are only hurting each other and themselves by adopting adversarial roles. While Americans are fighting with each other, the rest of the world will walk right by us economically.

Anonymous reply, competitiveness survey,
Harvard Business Review, Sept./Oct. 1987.

We've reached a point where most people recognize the need for change, but no one wants to pay the price. The stockholders want to increase their return on investment, management wants to increase their income and profit share, and the union wants to bring their members a bigger piece of the pie. However, the size of the pie is getting smaller due to an increase in the number of competitors and the improvement of technology. There has to be a paradigm shift in the underlying structure. A shared vision needs to be developed that addresses the honest concerns of all stakeholders. An honest assessment of current reality must be the foundation. Technology and innovation are reducing the number of hours needed to build a car. This means fewer employees, both hourly and salaried. Union and management need to recognize this reality and work jointly on making the adjustments with the interests of the work force in mind.

It's my opinion that collective bargaining is absolutely essential in this country. It's also my opinion that unions need to make a paradigm shift to survive in a global marketplace. Unions need to rethink their reason for existence and reconsider their role in today's marketplace. A myriad of issues relevant to today's current reality need to be considered: Quality, customer satisfaction, pricing, production costs, overhead, health care, employee mental and physical well-being, diversity, training and re-training, re-structuring jobs, flexibility in jobs, different levels of union responsibility to members (part time employees), and shared jobs, to name a few. Without these changes, unions will win some battles, but they will lose the war.

Management needs to reconsider their traditional view of unions as an obstacle to productivity and profit. Honesty in communications and negotiations is a good start. A recognition of the union experience and expertise as a valuable resource would be a nice shift. Creating avenues to resources, allowing the unions to address many of the overwhelming challenges that face businesses and industrial plants today, would reap great rewards.

And last, but certainly not least, a fair distribution of profits is needed; one that not only rewards the experience and skill of management, but also recognizes the talents, creativity, and skills contributed by the labor force.

As I travel across the country to work with educational institutions, social service agencies, correctional systems and industrial plants, I've come to believe that every good job that goes off-shore, or disappears because of union/management difficulties, contributes to our decline as a society. We must find a way to work through disagreements and challenges without the union/management issues costing jobs or market share. When you get two people alone, without politics, position or power involved, both parties will agree that we need to make these significant changes in the way we do business to compete and survive. It's the doing that's the problem. It will take a major paradigm shift to get from where we are now, steeped in tradition, to where we need to be — flexible learning organizations. In healthy organizations, every employee, both union and management, is valued and works toward a vision that maximizes all of the strengths and talents within the organization.

True transformation will not occur within a company unless it is rooted in the belief that every man and woman who works for the company is its greatest asset and those assets must, at all times, be treated with dignity and respect.

Thomas L. Weekley, Jay C. Wilber,
United We Stand, 1996.

My years with the U.A.W. and General Motors have allowed me to work with many of the plants across the country. There is no one answer that will transform this huge organization; one-size-fits-all won't work. Each plant and each local union presents its own unique challenges. For instance, NUMMI (New United Motors Manufacturing Inc.) and Hamtramck are two totally different worlds; the Corvette plant in Bowling Green, Kentucky poses different challenges than a plant in Arlington, Texas. Some differences relate to the geographical area where the plant is located. The product being produced has an impact on the culture of the plant; the local leadership of the union and the local management team can have major impacts on the plant's survival. Still, the one common issue is people; the relationship between labor and management, and their willingness to take a proactive approach to change.

It is essential that the U.A.W. and General Motors re-evaluate everything that goes on in their world. The U.A.W.'s Solidarity House and General Motor's Corporate Headquarters need to take the lead in this effort. Everybody wants to go to heaven, but nobody wants to die. Everyone wants to improve quality and reduce overhead, but nobody wants it to impact their department, their plant, their people, their bonuses, or their overtime. There's lots of rhetoric but not much real change.

There are no automobile workers more skilled than the men and women at General Motors.

There's no automobile company in the world with a more talented and knowledgeable management group. The technology and sophistication in product design and development is unequaled in the industry. General Motors has everything needed to produce the highest quality, most competitive automobiles on the market. The Cadillac, Chevrolet, Buick, Oldsmobile, and Pontiac should offer consumers the best choice at the best price. Somehow this huge corporation fell behind in their response to change. However, there has been a consistent improvement in quality and a constant effort to be more responsive to the desires of the consumer.

The one area that has General Motors and the U.A.W. deadlocked is how to reduce the number of man-hours it takes to put a car in a dealer's showroom. The automobile industry went through decades of abundance, years and years when General Motors could sell everything that came off the end of an assembly line. The price and quality of cars was uncontested. This was Nirvana for both salaried employees and the United Auto Workers. Work expanded and new titles were established. The process became self perpetuating by both union and management as the U.A.W. became a powerful bureaucracy, and General Motor's corporate management grew into a cumbersome, insulated group of suits and ties disconnected from the business of producing quality automobiles. No management person or shop steward decided to bring about this dilemma, it simply evolved. Then one day the wheel fell off...the consumer was offered choices! A series of major paradigm shifts changed our world. Hondas, Toyotas, Datsuns, Nissans and Audis began to fill showrooms. General Motors and the U.A.W. were brought face to face with their creation. All of the perks that people had grown accustomed to were challenged. Quality, customer satisfaction, product design, consumer awareness, and the involvement of employees became front burner issues. Change has become the battle cry from Michigan to California.

How do you take back what has become normal, expected compensation? When overtime is a requirement to meet your financial obligations, it becomes a major obstacle to change. How do you change work rules that have become obsolete, or implement flexibility when the change threatens seniority? How do you do all of these things in an organization represented by the strongest union in the world and controlled by management who have had little or no actual involvement in the workforce? The necessary changes would need to be accepted and supported by union leaders whose political future may rest on their decision. Total support needs to be demonstrated by managers whose power base would be at risk and who realize that their very position may be eliminated. This is a tough sell! But, without a major paradigm shift, General Motors will continue to lose market share and the U.A.W. will continue to lose members.

This challenge is not unique to General Motors and the United Autoworkers. Every organization, both union and non-union, is faced with similar challenges. The good news is that the changes necessary can be accomplished if all parties decide to work towards the same end result. A good example is Plain Talk Printing, a small printing company in Des Moines, Iowa. This is one of the few unionized printing companies in the area, and yet they can beat most other printing companies in price, quality and on-time delivery. Their pay scale for employees is higher than many non-union shops. But because of their willingness to cooperate and recognize that there's only one way to approach the future, and that is in a win-win relationship, they are a vibrant, profitable company.

5. Champions Of Change

Change is such an ambiguous word. For those who are employees in corporations, the word carries with it unclear messages wrapped in a history of downsizing, plant closures, and negative experiences. For the individual, the word change brings back memories of learning, relearning, exercise cards, diets, moving vans, and stress. It should be no surprise that we resist the idea of change.

Over the past twenty-five years, I've been blessed with opportunities to participate in a wide range of efforts to initiate change. These run the gamut from large unionized industrial plants to small independent companies; from sales groups to

CPA's; from government agencies to inner cities; and from law enforcement to prisons. In every case, if the change effort has any chance of success, it rests on the energies of a few internal champions.

Champions come in all forms. They can be CEO's, union leaders, middle management, line staff, mayors, public officials, parents, teenagers, correctional officers, or inmates. They all share a desire to make the world a better place. They recognize the need for change.

Champions of change have an awareness and a belief that they can make a difference. They also understand that to build support for a change initiative, it needs to be an interest-based approach. The interests of all stakeholders should be included prior to deciding a course of action.

Champions of change also have to be tenacious and resilient. At the outset of any change initiative the resistance can be formidable. The nay-sayers emerge from the most unlikely places, and without strong support, the negativity can squelch the spirit of even the most committed champions.

When we begin to implement our Framework for Change process inside an organization, one of the first steps is to build support for the process so the champions of change are not alone in their efforts. This support needs to come from leadership first; top-level managers and union leaders (if the organization is unionized) need to be involved and supportive.

Champions are often left holding the bag because management does not follow through on their commitments, or because union leaders are not willing to stand up for what's right. I've found that the larger the organization, the more difficult it becomes to get long-term support for champions. Corporate executives and government leaders are often disconnected from what goes on at the local plant or agency. Commitments are made and broken with seemingly little concern for its impact on local managers and union leaders. The truth gets clouded in contract language until it becomes almost impossible to determine accountability for specific action.

In spite of the external pressure, true champions of change continue to work toward the goal of improving the lives of people in their organizations and communities.

Ten years ago, General Motors and the United Auto Workers (U.A.W.) formed an alliance called the Quality Network. This was an interest-based approach to change. There is interest and value to all General Motors and U.A.W. employees in improving the quality of their products. The Quality Network is a process designed to improve communication and relationships between union and salaried employees, using quality as a vehicle.

Champions for this process were developed across the General Motors system. Jay Wilber, management's representative at the corporate level, and Tom Weekley, Jay's U.A.W. counterpart, have been championing this process for many years. Because of their interest in finding a new paradigm for General Motors and the U.A.W., Tom and Jay co-authored a book entitled, "United We Stand." The book talks about the need to re-evaluate how the two entities do business together. They have established, at the plant level, two representatives from salaried and two from hourly, called the Quad Four. Their responsibility is to champion the integration of the systems and strategies of the Quality Network into the corporate culture. At the plant level, however, unless there is top-level leadership support that is willing to deal with issues honestly and above the board, the Quad Four champions of change are left with an uphill battle. Progress is slow, but the true champions roll with the punches and continue to support the initiatives that will keep the men and women at General Motors employed.

Across the country I've met men and women who are making a difference. One of my greatest joys is to take our Framework for Change training to a company, whether live or through our facilitated video process, and witness the birth of a new champion.

Somehow the awareness of our power to make a difference gets buried under life's difficulties. What was once a fire is slowly extinguished by setbacks, disappointments, and violations of trust, but the ember still lives in our souls. For some, the

Framework for Change process seems to blow away the residue and rekindle the fire. This happens in shipyards, pharmaceutical plants, inner cities, and in prisons. When the fire is re-ignited, it starts a chain reaction and the flames can bring a community back to life.

East Palo Alto, California is a prime example. The mayor of that city, Sharifa Wilson, saw the fire in David Lewis, a former gang leader. By uniting their energies, and through their courage and commitment, the people were ignited into action that transformed the city.

I've had the same experience in prisons where the warden, associate warden, correctional staff and inmates have come together and created an environment where positive change could occur.

To champion change the first step should be to communicate clearly, with everyone in the organization, the purpose for the change process. This should be done with an interest-based approach. The common interests of all parties involved must be identified. It's extremely important that the communication be open and honest in order to build trust and support. In our substance abuse program, *A Framework for Recovery*, the participants are asked at the end of each session to sign an "Agreement with Myself"; we tell them, "Don't sign it if you don't mean it!" So, don't say you'll do something if you're not going to follow through. Most people will support a change initiative if they understand the reasons for the process, and are assured that their interests have been considered.

The change initiative should always be undertaken with the intent of improving both the culture of and the performance of the organization. I believe that the change training itself should be based on self-discovery. By allowing individuals to participate in a self-discovery process, a sense of personal ownership is created. As a result, most people feel empowered rather than attacked or criticized.

The challenge for many people involved in a change process is tying their efforts to bottom line results. There's no question that change needs to have an impact on the bottom line. This keeps a company competitive and provides job security for employees. But, sometimes it's difficult to show the relationship between what is referred to as "soft skills" training and the profit and loss statement. Champions of change recognize how these seemingly intangible benefits relate to the bottom line.

The employee who has been trading time for money suddenly becomes productive; sick leave is reduced because stress is reduced. Results come in many forms: grievances that aren't filed, heart attacks that don't happen, creativity that comes from a sense of ownership of the things that *do* happen. A committee person and a supervisor might learn to take a proactive approach to resolving a potential conflict. A sexual harassment lawsuit doesn't occur because a person becomes aware that dignity and respect for each individual is a non-negotiable item. An employee will suddenly come to work with a different attitude because his or her personal relationships have improved. Accidents decrease because people feel a personal stake in the business.

These are the bottom line payoffs that happen when culture change takes place in an organization. This kind of result is hard to measure on a financial statement and difficult to explain at a stockholder's meeting. But these are the things that make up the breakfast for champions of change. These are the rewards that keep them in the game. Profitability is important, but it's these intangibles that fuel the engine for change agents. It's making the world a better place.

When positive change starts taking place in an environment it seems to create a ripple effect. This was the case in Deschutes County, located in the high desert country of central Oregon. Ten years ago, Jerry Andres became CEO of Eagle Crest Resort in Redmond, and became a champion for positive change in the community. I was given the opportunity to bring our change training to their organization. During the course of these past few years, Eagle Crest has bloomed into a beautiful destination resort. Centered around two 18-hole golf courses, the resort includes condominiums, a hotel, and a conference center. The area includes rivers and a snow capped mountain range that offers the best snow skiing in the country. Most important, however, is that Eagle Crest has created a community spirit that has ignited champions of change in schools, community agencies, and in the criminal justice arena.

Dennis Maloney who heads up the juvenile corrections division is a great example of what can happen when you believe that change is possible. Mr. Maloney recognized that what was happening in juvenile justice was not serving the needs of the community, the victims, the juvenile offender, nor was it increasing public safety. With the involvement of law enforcement, public officials and the business community, Dennis has been a catalyst for creating a paradigm shift in the way young offenders are managed.

First he realized that the resources had to be available at the community level. In Oregon it costs approximately $46,000 a year to keep a juvenile offender in a state facility. When the year's sentence is completed, the young person returns to his or her community, and often they return with little chance for long-term success.

Recognizing this fact, Dennis pioneered a piece of legislation that turned the process on its ear. Deschutes County sentenced, on the average, thirty young people per year to state facilities, at a cost of approximately one million, five hundred thousand dollars per year. Mr. Maloney convinced the state to agree to give Deschutes County a community block grant for $46,000 times 30, or one and a half million dollars. Now if the County has to send a juvenile to the state, they send the offender and $46,000. However, if they can deal with the offender in the community, they have the $46,000 to develop programs and support. Forty-six thousand dollars can fund a program benefiting many for an entire year.

They also passed a bond measure in Deschutes County to build a comprehensive community justice center. This center includes a lock-up facility, coupled with treatment, education, parental support, and an opportunity for restorative justice. The offender can give back to the community and the victims are included in the process. The champions for change in Deschutes County, Oregon may well have created a model that works. Now wouldn't that be a unique experience! I've had the opportunity to bring our Framework for Change into this exciting project.

Across the country there are projects that are driven by champions of positive change; I feel blessed and honored to be involved in many of these efforts. This book, *Change is an Inside Job*, recognizes and is a tribute to those men and women who are driven by the desire to make a difference. There are many who are working to make the world a better place.

Part Two
It Seems to Me...

It Seems To Me...

The Key To Good Relationships Is Honoring Each Other's Windows To The World.

6. Windows

It seems to me that we see the world through our own individual window to the world. It's like a pair of glasses that are always there in front of our eyes. Every time we turn our head, the glasses are there to improve our perception of things around us. The difference between a pair of glasses and our personal window to the world is that we can remove the glasses, but the window is internal. It's been developed over time through our experiences, information we've accepted from experts (self-proclaimed in many cases), the knowledge we've acquired in school, from professors, friends and co-workers, until it solidifies into our window. It's there when we turn our heads. It affects our decisions and our behavior.

Black is black and white is white to most of us, but it's the areas of gray that cause most of our problems. Through the eyes of a child, the world is an awesome, exciting adventure, something to explore and to marvel at. But, to many adults, the world is no longer exciting and the wonders have been drowned by unhappiness and disappointment. It's the same world, but the window has gradually changed and what was once adventure becomes drudgery. Eventually, life loses its luster.

When we understand that our own perceptions of the world are determined by our past experiences and the influence of other people, then we can begin to understand that that's also true for the people we live with and work with. Once we are able to respect each other's perceptions we can begin to build meaningful dialogues that are based on trust and respect.

People have different perceptions about change. For some people, change creates excitement and anticipation. For others, change is fearful and people will fight to maintain the status quo. The difference in how we experience change lies in our view of the world. So as we begin this section, I would ask the reader to understand that these are my perceptions, based on my background and my experiences. As you have discovered, my window to the world may differ from yours.

I grew up on the streets and my mentors were safecrackers and burglars. During that time of my life they became my family, and the illegal behaviors were just normal activities. Over time I became a safecracker, although not a very good one or I wouldn't have gotten busted so many times. I served seventeen years in maximum security prisons. I've been shot and stabbed, I've been in riots, I've escaped, I've done a year in The Hole on bread and water. I've made major changes in my life and am now an honest human being. I've been heavily involved in union/management training for 15 years. I work with government, inner cities, and in prisons. I've had a triple bypass, I've had cancer, I've been married, raised three children, been divorced, remarried, and now have 10 grandchildren. I've designed many video-based training programs, and I'm a student of human behavior. Change is possible.

Each of us have been conditioned over time to see the world in our own unique way. Sometimes it's impossible to understand why others don't see things as we do. I guess that's what makes life so exciting at times and so frustrating at other times. But the biggest challenge we face is to recognize that we don't always see the truth, but rather our interpretation of the truth.

By staying open to new ideas and being willing to listen to other people's perspectives, our window to the world enlarges, gets clearer, and life becomes a much more joyful experience.

It Seems To Me...

We Need To Create An Honesty Movement Where A Handshake Means A Deal Is A Deal.

7. Honesty

It seems to me that honesty, as a cultural value, has been relegated to the archives of times long past. Having grown up in a dishonest world, I am very familiar with a culture where dishonesty is the norm. But, to find it so pervasive in the world I live in today causes me great concern. The old adage that "honesty pays" would be hard to prove in many of the places I visit. Lying, stretching the truth, cheating, manipulation, cover-ups, breaking contracts, and not living up to our word are so commonplace that they hardly cause a moment's concern. There was a time when a handshake was all that was needed to seal a deal. Today, when you reach out to shake hands, your other hand better be on your wallet.

Everyday, the front pages of newspapers across the country are filled with stories of dishonesty: extramarital affairs, illegal contributions to political candidates, misusing pension funds, fraud by government leaders, cover-ups by corporations, kickbacks, and on and on. How can we expect our young people to embrace honesty when we're not giving them the proper role models? When money becomes the overriding principle, it becomes easier and easier to rationalize questionable tactics and behavior. It's little wonder that honesty has lost its value.

I'm sure honesty is still alive and well in many segments of society, but it doesn't reach the newspapers or the tabloids.

Dishonesty is pervasive in many corporations and in most of our cities. The concept of an honest day's work for an honest day's pay may still sell in some remote areas of the country, but it's not reality in most of our corporations. "How can I get the most money for the least amount of effort?" plays better in industrial U.S.A. The idea that an individual's contribution to the corporate goal is vital to its overall success has been lost in the drive for increased profits where employees are perceived merely as a means to an end. Unions, like management, get caught up in the quest for power and dollars, and lose sight of the membership. This gradually creates a culture where people feel disconnected from the corporation or company. When it reaches this stage, dishonesty is easy to rationalize.

The measure of a man's real character is what he would do if he knew he would never be found out.
Thomas Macaulay, English writer/statesman

When I was growing up on the streets, I felt disconnected from society. Then, as I began my experience as a consumer of correctional services, I felt even more disconnected. I wasn't a part of society; I belonged to a subculture. When you don't belong to society, it's easy to rationalize stealing and dishonesty. When people feel disconnected from a company or corporation, it is easy to rationalize taking from the organization. This can take the form of just showing up but not working, or manipulating the job so it creates overtime. People rationalize dishonesty when they abuse sick leave or medical claims, or misuse corporate property. This holds true of both management and hourly employees. It becomes the norm and we blind ourselves to it through rationalization.

Many of the residents of inner cities that have been allowed to deteriorate and become urban ghettos feel disconnected from society. Welfare and government programs are manipulated, misused and abused by people who feel cheated and locked out of the American dream. America's promise of life, liberty and the pursuit of happiness has lost its meaning in many segments of society. To many people, the future looks hopeless. Dishonesty, hustling and stealing can become a way of life when survival, as a subculture, becomes the day to day reality. Some of the most creative people I've met are welfare recipients who have mastered the art of beating the system. Feeling disconnected from the government that allocates the money and establishes the guidelines, it's easy to rationalize the dishonest, devious behavior. "They don't give a sh— about us so why should I give a damn?" is a common response if you question their behavior.

Honesty pays, but, damn, it's a hard sell! I've worked hard at honesty over the years and it's been a struggle competing honestly against people who give kickbacks, wine and dine the potential buyer, and don't really care whether there is value to the individual. Holding on to honesty has made the game very interesting. But, it's now the only way I want to live. I've done it the other way and it may play well short-term, but results take time to measure. Eventually there are consequences.

I have great friends who represent leaders, stewards, and members that are honest, committed union brothers and sisters and I respect their efforts. I also have good friends who are managers of companies and corporations, that are honest, committed leaders who care about the employees in the corporation. I have many friends who live in inner cities, some who survive on welfare, that are honest, caring people who feel a part of society and reach out to their neighbors. So it's not all negative out there.

Honesty is still alive and well in the majority of society, but it doesn't sell newspapers and the tabloids won't pay for it. As I see it, we need to create an honesty movement that will return us to a place where a handshake means a deal is a deal. Treating people with the dignity and respect they deserve as human beings can help restore them to honesty. When we stop setting up systems that force people to cheat in order to survive, they will stop. These kinds of changes will not happen overnight; it is a gradual and incremental process. However, sometimes it is necessary to simply take the moral highroad, no matter what other people are doing, simply because it is the right thing to do.

It Seems To Me...

The Question "What's The Right Thing To Do?" Has Been Replaced By "What Can I Get Away With?

8. Cultural Paradoxes

It seems to me that what gets rewarded is what gets done. I've looked back at my own life experiences using this perspective as a measuring stick. Having grown up in a prison culture where manipulation and dishonesty were the norm, it's quite obvious why the inmate gradually learns to manipulate and play the game that has been ingrained in the environment. The inmates who are the best at playing the convict game generally get the best jobs, are afforded the most privileges and, based on sentencing guidelines, will be the first to be released.

They are the ones who experience the least hardship in doing their time. Now, how would I know this? Because I learned the game and became a master at manipulating the system. The men and women who just do their time and are unable, not smart enough, or unwilling to play the game, do the hardest time and generally do more time. This is a fact of life inside the majority of prisons in this country.

There's no judgment involved in my analysis, this is just the way the game is played. What gets rewarded, is what gets done. The question, "What's the right thing to do?" has been replaced by "What can I get away with?" There are certain principles that are dictated by the culture. Most so-called "good convicts" will strictly adhere to these unwritten principles. They include, but are not limited to, the following: You don't snitch, you can steal from The Man but not fellow convicts, you don't fraternize with the correctional officers, you back the play of your partners, and your word is good to your specific circle of friends. There are other principles that center around race, type of crime, type of criminal, etc., but these are more specific to certain groups and seem to be less of a reality in today's world. The world of prisons is a world where dishonesty is expected. The convicts know this, and the staff knows this, so there's no real surprise on anyone's part if a dishonest act occurs.

I left that world in 1971. When I first became aware of my own responsibilities as a citizen and learned that thinking skills could be applied to make changes in my life, one of the things I made a conscious decision about was honesty. I'd always been a good convict. I was honest within the framework of a prison, but now I wanted to be an honest person within the framework of society.

I've incorporated some basic principles that have served me well over the years. My word is good. I make it a point to be on time. I keep my appointments. If I make a commitment, I follow through. I pay my debts (at times it's taken me a while, but I always pay). I try to treat everyone with respect. I always do the best job I can do. I contribute to the less fortunate, especially men and women in prison. I don't cheat and I don't steal. Now let me say that I'm also human and make mistakes. In fact, I have a master's degree in making mistakes. I try not to make the same ones, but I'm sure I have, and probably will again. These are all pretty basic principles, but they are principles that I have had to incorporate into myself. They are principles that are learned behaviors that anyone can learn to apply in their own life.

The reason I've asked you, the reader, to look at the concept, "what gets rewarded is what gets done" is to explore some of the things that have occurred gradually and incrementally in our industrial plants, our communities and our society. The culture of an organization drives performance. We have established systems in many cases that encourage and reward manipulation, and in some cases, a subtle form of dishonesty. My background comes from this kind of culture, so when I see manipulation, I recognize it. When dishonesty appears clothed in corporate or union attire, I can see through the disguise in that arena as well.

There's a time-worn adage that says, "honesty pays." But does it really? Or have we gradually allowed the principle of honesty to become a barrier to success? The old American philosophy of "an honest day's work for an honest day's pay" has been all but lost in the plants that I visit. What gets rewarded, is what gets done!

Health care and insurance costs continue to rise. We have created systems that penalize the honest person and reward those that scream the loudest and longest. There's a story about a bus driver with seven passengers on his bus who ran into a car parked by the curb. The driver, concerned about the people in the car, jumped out of the bus and rushed to the automobile he'd hit. Fortunately, no one was injured. When he got back on his bus he had *thirty* passengers! Litigation has become the golden parachute. However, don't wait to call a lawyer regardless of the extent of your injuries. A friend of mine was rear-ended by an uninsured driver with no brakes. She was shaken up by the accident, but seemed to be alright, therefore she failed to contact an attorney and tried to resolve the matter in an honest way. Several months later, her neck was still bothering her and it was determined that she had injured her neck and there was some neurological damage. Her own insurance company was now unwilling to respond, so my friend engaged an attorney. The struggle goes on as I write this chapter. She has been subject to a never-ending series of tests, and stacks of forms that ask for information from ten years past. Both my friend and the attorney are worn out by the process.

I read John Grisham's book, "The Rainmaker." It's the story of a large insurance company that ignored the plight of a young man dying of a terminal illness, until a young lawyer brings the insurance company to its knees. This story is played out in the real world on a smaller scale every day. If there is ever a next time, my friend would be wise to scream about neck and back pains all the way to the hospital with her lawyers at work in the ambulance. Does honesty pay? Apparently not everywhere, all the time.

There has been a gradual shift from work that adds value to the end product that a plant produces to positions that add overhead but no real value. This practice has evolved to an art form in today's plants. Positions exist that perpetuate themselves just by their existence. Overtime has become a necessity for employees to maintain a lifestyle that was created by overtime in the first place. Why would anyone want to complete a job on time and risk losing their boat or car? Even the naïve might suspect some manipulation is likely to occur in these situations.

How far do practices like these go before a hint of dishonesty creeps into the equation? What gets rewarded is what gets done! What possible rewards do employees receive if they eliminate overtime for men and women who have families that rely on the extra dollars? Is it honest to reward top level managers who have not contributed to the overall good of the plant? How do we justify to employees working on the line all of the non-value added activities that have become the norm in today's industrial world? Meetings, teams, benchmarking, and visioning proliferate in the culture of many of today's organizations. It has become an addiction, where benchmarkers are benchmarking the benchmarkers. Who is doing the work? Six-month leaves to evaluate best practices are undertaken only to discover that the employees reject the new procedures and the process starts anew. This is not to say that these types of activities have no value, but when they lose sight of the true reason for their existence and function as an entity in and of themselves, then they should be put to rest.

Trust is the cornerstone of any healthy long-term relationship. Trust develops through consistency; people doing what they say they will do. If, through no fault of their own, they are unable to follow through, then open, honest communication with the other parties is critical. Trust lies at the heart of the paradox of union/management relationships. Union leaders are well aware of top management's responsibilities to the stockholder. The value of shares to the stockholder is the real report card of how well a company is managed. Union leaders know that top level managers are also stockholders, so the executive's job is to reduce costs and increase profits. In most cases, this will include the reduction of man-hours in a finished product, which means jobs to people. Top level management knows that the union leadership's role is to get top dollar for their members, make the jobs easier, satisfy the needs of the most vocal members and the malcontents, keep jobs in the plant and get re-elected. These are incongruous roles at best. The cultural paradox at play is that one group's "best interests" are at odds with the other group's "best interests" and, as long as that conflict continues, the "best interests" of the organization of which they're a part, can never be served. Without trust and a willingness to manage conflict in a positive way, the union/management relationships will continue to be an ongoing battle that neither side can win.

Because of the seemingly impossible situation, subtle forces of manipulation and dishonesty creep into the workplace. Management will throw a bone to the union in the form of setting up a team or committee that will include some of the most vocal union members. This usually includes a few perks like time off the job, lunches or dinners, and a trip or two. The leadership of the union might go off-site with management for a retreat, complete with booze, food, and a laugh or two. These kinds of activities generally buy a couple of months without major conflict, then the perks are forgotten and management is once again perceived as a bunch of S.O.B.'s, and the union leaders are regarded as a bunch of thugs out to bankrupt the company. In the midst of this bizarre relationship are the labor relations people, who are usually lawyers with long-term job security so long as things don't get solved. However, this inability to work together also requires a large organizational development group working on graphs, timelines, and setting up teams, committees, and a corporate vision. Then there are personnel who interact with labor relations and the organizational development people who have the responsibility of moving people around, solving personnel problems, and serving as counselors and intermediaries. The inability to get along has gradually allowed internal empires to be established with no clear, direct connection to the development of a product or service.

A small plant in the south with only five hundred employees had an organizational development department with eight or ten full-time people. They had their own separate offices, national reputations as gurus in self-directed teams and yet minimal connection to the employees in the plant! How does this happen? It happens through a subtle form of manipulation by someone who knows how to play the game.

Somewhere in the evolution of this phenomenon, honesty and integrity have been lost. The void has been filled by dishonesty, manipulation, conflict, and attorneys. We have established systems that invite people to cheat and act in dishonest ways. Many times I've seen managers who were forced to operate in the gray areas of honesty to get the job done. The bidding process is a prime example. A manager knows what he or she needs in terms of training or a specific product, but they are forced to put it up for bid. To avoid being required to accept a product that does not meet their needs, managers will manipulate the bidding process. Just getting a purchase order through the maze of bureaucracy will deter most managers.

The welfare system has created a training ground for manipulation. "What gets rewarded, is what gets done." A young divorced mother with two children on welfare is caught in a vicious trap. Her health care, day care, and food stamps are tied to the umbilical cord of welfare. There's no way she can secure a job that will replace these life necessities. We are beginning to build some bridges that will aid the transition from welfare to work, but welfare has spawned dishonesty in segments of society that feel disconnected from the American dream.

Time and time again, when I work with organizations and talk to people about how systems are constantly manipulated, their response is, "But that's the way it's always been done." My message to them is that it doesn't have to continue to be that way. Change is possible, but it's a choice we make. We can choose to realign our systems to reflect core values of honesty and integrity. We can choose to treat people fairly, with dignity and respect. When we make the choice to change the way we do business and how we treat people, gradually and incrementally, the "way we've always done things" becomes unacceptable.

Men of integrity, by their very existence, rekindle the belief that, as a people, we can live above the level of moral squalor.

John Gardner/Author

For this country to remain a world leader, we must return to some basic principles. Honesty is the foundation for a strong society. It's the only way union and management can survive long-term. Employees need to be compensated fairly, treated

with dignity and respect, given equal access to opportunities and be told the truth. In turn, employees need to give back an honest contribution to the
company or corporation. Management and union
leadership each need to be honest and follow
through on commitments. When an agreement is
reached or a contract signed, both sides need to
honor the document. If conflicts arise, deal with
them openly and honestly, and don't let the conflict
destroy the agreement. If both sides would agree to
these principles, a foundation of trust could be built.
A new industrial world can be built on a foundation
of trust.

It Seems To Me...

Litigation Is No Longer The Last Resort; It's A First Resort Motivated By **Money**.

9. A Litigious Society

It seems to me that litigation has become the first resource in solving our problems. There are over one million lawyers in the United States, and the number continues to grow. In Japan, a country one-half the population of the United States, there are fewer than thirty thousand attorneys. We have become a society that sues at the drop of a hat, or a hot cup of coffee. This frenzied drive to file a lawsuit cuts across economics, religion, politics, race, gender, and even reaches into the bowels of our prisons. The legal profession is the beneficiary of this drive to right wrongs through financial recompense, and therefore promotes the process. The legal profession has one of the strongest lobbying groups in Washington D.C. It seems to me that every new law that is adopted by politicians on The Hill increases the opportunities for lawyers. Today lawyers advertise their services through television, newspapers, and billboards. You can even find advertisements for attorneys who will defend you against a ticket for driving under the influence of alcohol posted above the urinals in the restrooms of taverns and bars.

When I was caught up in the criminal justice system, my awareness of the legal profession was limited to prosecutors and defense attorneys. The quality of your defense attorney depended on your ability to pay! If you had been on the streets long enough to accumulate some cash, you'd hire the best attorney your money could buy. If you were broke, which most of the guys who wind up in prison are, then you had to settle for a public defender. Families sometimes bankrupt themselves to pay for an attorney to defend a son, daughter, or other relative who had no chance of being found "not guilty." The hustlers and thieves in a city know which attorneys have the best connections and the best chance of beating a case. Professional criminals set aside money to hire an attorney in case they get busted. It's a business expense. In the thief's mind, the courts are a place where you can always make a deal if the money is right. The lawyer is the deal maker. This side of the legal profession can be indifferent and insensitive when it comes to justice.

Over the past two decades, the criminal justice system has become more and more a bartering system. Lawyers and prosecutors are the brokers. "If my client testifies against his or her co-defendants, what can you offer?", the defendant's attorney begins the negotiation. Another scenario that takes place goes like this: "If you put my client on the streets, he or she will give you a major dealer!" Or, "If my client pleads guilty to this lesser offense, will you drop all other charges?" Justice is lost in this process and the reality is that much of what happens to you in court depends on your ability to give up other people. Clients know that the one who gets down first wins. The one who testifies against his or her partner, or agrees to give up names of some other lawbreaker is the one who is set free or given a much lighter sentence. This has gradually eroded the integrity of the criminal justice system. It not only diminishes the respect by the criminal element, it also impacts the respect by law enforcement officers. The real loser in this charade is the community that finds itself victim to criminals who have been put back on the street, not because they have been changed or rehabilitated, but because they have turned against another person.

During my years in prison I met some attorneys who were ethical and truly worked for justice. Some were highly paid and some were public defenders. I also met some lawyers who were as crooked as the clients they were defending and justice didn't enter into their job description. This was my background and experience when I began to interact with society at large. I thought that lawyers and the legal profession were a part of my past. Boy, was I mis-taken.

Today, close to three decades later, I'm appalled by the impact lawyers and litigation have on our lives. In the corporate world, a team of lawyers is essential to survival. While a company is produc-ing and distributing products, lawsuits are being fought in courtrooms to defend the company's right to sell their wares. Every day of the week lawsuits are being filed against corporations' internal prac-tices. Illegal hiring, illegal firing, sex discrimination, racial injustice, sexual harassment, same sex harass-ment, product deficiencies, price fixing, monopolies, unfair bidding practices, the list goes on into infin-ity. This is Nirvana for the legal profession. There are lawyers on both sides of the issue. Both sets of attorneys are being compensated — win, lose or draw. The resources that are used to pay legal fees come out of the labor of employees in the plant. The dollars spent are gone; they put nothing back into the future of the company. There are no new jobs, no new equipment, and no increase in salaries. It is a cost of doing business that becomes a catch twenty-two. You can't live with attorneys and you can't live without them.

An attorney's existence depends on conflict. There will always be a need for an attorney. But there needs to be a return to sanity in regards to liti-gation. When an adult of sound mind gives up his or her personal responsibility, and then sues because of their decision, something's out of balance.

In my mind, the loss of personal
accountability is one of the major
problems plaguing our corporations;
our schools; our entire society.
GG

Schools, non-profit organizations, charities, and religious institutions are at-risk without legal counsel. The open warfare by attorneys willing to take on even the most bizarre cases in hopes of an out-of-court settlement has created a paranoia in boardrooms across the country. It has also cast suspicion on those cases that are legitimate complaints against unjust practices. Insurance companies that refuse to pay legitimate claims feed into the nightmare of litigation. Unethical managers and illegal hiring practices contribute to the fees paid to attorneys. Misuse of public resources and discrimination by bigots creates a field day for litigation attorneys. There are hundreds of reasons for the increase in lawyers and litigation. But, if I could name one thing that has had the biggest impact on the thriving world of lawyers and the legal profession, it would be money, with a capital "M". Gradually and incrementally, we have gotten used to a legal system that revolves around money, not justice. It's a game with a huge up side and a very small down side. There are huge dollars to be made in the world of lawsuits. The cigarette industry alone has paid out billions of dollars in legal fees over the past ten years. The right legal claim combined with the right legal representation can mean retirement. The price of, and negative publicity attached to, going to court has caused many corporations to settle out of court regardless of guilt. On the other side of this equation is the price of taking a case to court. That price has caused many plaintiffs with legitimate claims to drop their lawsuits. An attorney is always involved and their fee comes off the top.

Attorneys are like a bad-tasting medicine — you hate to take it, but if you don't, you probably won't get well. I hate to pay legal fees, but if I don't, I can't protect my interests. Unlike the medicine, which cures you so you can stop taking it, the need for an attorney never ends.

Litigation has become a way of life. It's no longer a means to an end; it has become the end itself.

It Seems To Me...

The True
Measurement Of
Any Change
Initiative Will
Come From The
People On The
Front Line.

10. Follow-Through

It seems to me that one of our greatest challenges is following through on our commitments. I've had the good fortune to participate in a number of efforts to bring about change in organizations over the past twenty years. When a change initiative is first introduced, it stimulates a rash of activities. Committees are formed, goals and objectives established, meetings begin to take place, and a general direction begins to unfold. Top level leadership is usually visible on the front end of the change initiative, and there's a sense of excitement in those people who have been designated as change agents.

From this initial burst of energy, a number of things can happen, depending on the creativity and focus of the group. Some companies begin by benchmarking other companies. Teams visit other organizations searching for "best practices." This can take considerable time depending on how much money has been allocated for this effort!

Some companies begin their change initiatives by hiring a consultant. This might be in conjunction with the benchmarking process or it can be an independent decision. Consultants are always around, ready to come to the aid of companies that are trying to change. The consultant becomes a resource for initiating new practices, or for changing existing systems. Then there's always a certain amount of training that needs to take place prior to implementing the change initiative: problem solving, how to run a meeting, team building, communication skills, coaching, etc., etc.

By this time, they've used up a good portion of the budget and the initial enthusiasm that comes from new experiences has diminished. By the time they get to the implementation phase, the fun has gone out of the project. The leadership no longer comes to the meetings and it becomes more and more difficult to get the time and resources to implement all that you've learned. This is the point at which most change initiatives begin to fade into the company's archives and the well-trained change agents go on to start their own consulting firms.

When we start a change initiative with Framework for Change 2000, our first concern is an agreement with leadership to create an expectation of follow-through for the people in the company. One reason why so many people resist change initiatives is past experience with programs that are started with tremendous enthusiasm and then die an early death. When employees see management failing to follow through, it's easy for them to rationalize their own cynicism. They have justification for believing that this is just another fad that they can ride out.

Follow-through is the "breakfast of champions." Change is a long-term process. We have become conditioned to expect results to happen instantly. The reality is that results take time to measure! Pendulum change, the kind that gets ignited by some significant event, can be useful by jumpstarting a change initiative. But it will not support long-term change. When we follow through, we begin to experience small incremental changes in both people and practices. As paradigm shifts are allowed to take root, you find people cooperating more readily. People who seem to present constant problems gradually become productive, self-empowered employees. Managers become more consistent in giving people positive feedback. The culture creates an enjoyable workplace.

> **When you change your attitude, you change your behavior, giving people an opportunity to respond differently.**
> **GG**

The true measurement of any change initiative will come from the people on the front line. How do they respond? How do the new practices affect their lives? Has it made their jobs easier or more difficult? How has it impacted quality and profitability? Has it created a sense of contribution in the employees' work lives? Has it improved trust among the people? Full implementation of a change initiative takes commitment and follow-through. Most often, when we are engaged with a corporation, we are brought in because some other initiative has stalled. Initiatives that are mandated from the top down fail to engage the hearts and minds of all the people in the organization. When you add to that factor the lack of follow-through from previous initiatives, cynicism multiplies.

When people are in an atmosphere of trust, they'll put themselves at risk; only through risk is there growth...reward...self-confidence...leadership.
Tom Peters, *A Passion for Excellence.*

We all understand that follow-through is an essential part of maintaining physical health. You don't expect one workout to make you physically fit and then return to business as usual. It takes constant follow-through. Over the years I've found that if I don't pay attention to my health, one day I happen to glance at the scale and find I'm a heavyweight. The same thing is true in business. If I don't pay attention and follow through with my customers, I'll wake up one day and find that the customer has found another supplier. This is also true in our relationships. Follow-through and commitment are absolutely necessary to achieve anything of significance. But, in spite of this knowledge, we fail to practice it in our companies.

It seems to me that trust breaks down because we don't follow through on our commitments.

It seems to me that prisons would be less likely to instill trust than a corporation. But, as I look back at my experiences in life, I'm not so sure this is true. The prison culture has an established code of behavior. Distorted as it might be, it seems more consistent than many other areas. This code has nothing to do with society's laws and norms; it is unique to the prison environment. A convict cannot go around snitching on other inmates and survive. You can't spread false rumors and walk the yard without repercussions. You can't give your word or make a commitment and then not follow through, and still expect to be accepted by your peers. These are unwritten laws and while they may be distorted in society's eyes, they are adhered to by most of the prison population.

We need to follow through on our commitments. We need to be focused and flexible at the same time. Follow-through is an essential ingredient in establishing trust. Trust creates an environment where change is regarded as a natural process for maintaining a competitive position in the market place.

It Seems To Me...

You Can, Through The Power Of Words And The Spirit Behind Them, Either Give People Heart, Or You Can Take Away Their Heart.

11. Communication

It seems to me that the words we use are not nearly as important as the spirit behind the word. Often we find people who know all the right words, but we know instinctively that they don't truly believe what they say.

I've had an opportunity to interact with a great model in communication skills. The President of Gordon Graham & Company and my wife, Eve Lenander, has a background in counseling and relationships, she has a degree in social work and has been involved with me in these activities since the mid-Eighties. Eve has the ability to communicate in a way that allows people to feel that she truly understands what they're saying and where they're coming from. Even her laughter comes from an honest place. Because of this, people really enjoy talking to her on the phone and interacting with her in the office. I'll find myself sometimes engrossed in a project and someone will come in and want to talk to me and I'll continue to work and say, "Go ahead, I'm listening." In reality, the individual knows that my mind is not on their concerns. When this happens, I'll often reflect back to Eve's skills, put down my work and give the person my full attention.

Eve came into my world by chance. I'd been separated and divorced for a number of years and was visiting some friends on New Year's Eve. Eve was there that evening. After that initial meeting, it took me a considerable amount of time to convince her that she should get to know me better. She had heard many of the wild stories that my friends enjoyed telling about my life on the streets, running Walla Walla with my fists, and all of the women that used to come in and out of my life. (Obviously, most of this was their imagination and not fact!) Eve grew up in Utah in Mormon country, and eventually settled in Seattle, as a single parent with two young sons. Her background is totally different than mine, yet we share many common values and desires. We both care about people and want to leave the world a little better place for our being here. Eve came to work with me as a facilitator of our video-based training programs. Her skills as a facilitator and her ability to communicate with diverse groups brought great value to our efforts across the United States. She proved to be equally capable of relating to inmates, union members, executive staff, and individuals.

Our relationship took tremendous energy on both our parts in order to reach a comfortable place. Eve prefers order, organization, preparation and neatness. I have a tendency to fix my bicycle while I ride it, and prepare on the run. In our home, Eve likes order — beds should be made, dishes put in the dishwasher, shoes in a shoe rack or a closet. I'm thinking, "What's the point?!" But because of our core values, our belief in change and people, and our love, we are able to work through these kinds of challenges and have established a healthy relationship. In my training sessions, I use an example that comes from my relationship with Eve. I ask the men in the room how many remember when they could dress themselves. I can be dressed and ready to go, and Eve will ask, "You're not going to wear that tie are you?" My response is, "Oh no, I've just got it on to decide how it looks in case I ever decide to wear it." Or, she will make the comment that, "those colors don't go together," and I'm thinking, "so, what's the point?" But we have gradually learned to work with each other in a way that allows us to move together down the road with a sense of harmony.

The spirit behind the words that we use with each other is a critical part of maintaining sound relationships. I like to use the story of the Wizard of Oz when we talk about the power of words. Dorothy and her three misfits, a tin man who had no heart, a straw man who had no brains, and a lion who had no courage, went off to seek the wizard who had the power to get Dorothy back to Kansas. This wizard happened to be a good wizard, and he said to the straw man, "The reason you don't have brains is because you don't have a diploma." He granted the straw man a diploma and transformed him. The Wizard told the lion, "The reason you don't have any courage is that you don't have any medals." He granted the lion a medal and the lion became courageous. He told the tin man, "The reason you don't have any heart is that you don't tick." He gifted the tin man with a clock that ticked, and the tin man had heart.

> **Through the power of words, you can give people heart, you can give them courage and you can give them brains. You can also, through the power of words, take away people's heart, take away their courage and take away their brains.**
>
> **GG**

It seems to me that we have an overabundance of negative wizards in the world today, and that what we need is a training ground to promote positive wizards who can bring about change in our organizations, our communities, and our families. Each of us is blessed with the power to impact other people. Eve has been a positive wizard in my life, and I would hope that I've been able to reciprocate. When the going gets rough, having the courage to apologize, ask forgiveness, forgive ourselves and move on is invaluable.

It Seems To Me...

A Vision Is Meaningless Unless It Engages The Hearts And Minds Of Employees At All Levels.

12. Fast Fixes

It seems to me that we have become addicted to practices and activities that were originally instituted to increase communications, improve quality and generate higher profits. Addiction is defined as compulsive behavior with short-term benefits and long-term destruction. With that in mind, I have noticed a tendency for individuals and organizations to become addicted to activities that start out as a means to an end, but in fact become an end in and of themselves. We implement committees, teams, benchmarking, and visioning to the point where you wonder, "Who's doing the work?"

Committees were originally designed to address problems or to create new methods of doing business. Teams were originally designed to bring a group of people together around a common goal.

Decision-making was then transferred to the team. Over time, even the most minute decisions were handed over to the team. This stifles individuals. "We can't make a decision until the team meets." Worse yet, teams are often given the responsibility of examining a situation, but no authority to act. Short-term, people feel empowered when they are part of a team. Over the long haul, though, giving people the illusion of responsibility without trusting them to take action is destructive.

Benchmarking, originally instituted to determine best practices, is running out of control in some companies and corporations. It's gotten to the point where companies are benchmarking the benchmarkers. Who wouldn't want to be on a benchmarking team that's traveling to some exotic location to benchmark another company or corporation? I've noticed that in the wintertime we prefer to benchmark in warm climates.

Visioning can become an addiction. We find it very difficult to function without a corporate vision. We devote hours and hours to creating mission statements that do little more than hang in corporate lobbies.

It would be interesting to conduct a study to determine the value added to an organization from all of these activities. There's no question that meetings are important, but if it's always the same people meeting with the same people talking about the other people, then meetings should be reevaluated. Teams certainly have a place in our organizations. But when the teams stifle the decision-making process and take away individuals' abilities to take action, then the team becomes an obstacle. Conversely, the unempowered team can become little more than a scapegoat. Benchmarking and best practices are excellent tools to determine how we match up, but after the benchmarking, someone needs to take action and implement the new practices. A vision can, in fact, bring some focus to individuals and organizations, but the visioning process is virtually meaningless unless it engages the hearts and minds of employees at all levels.

We are a fad-oriented society. In a world of sound-bite media, and instant everything, we have become addicted to the fast fix. When a new phrase or concept comes along, we jump on it like vultures. The phrase or concept takes off like wildfire. Up until the mid-Eighties, the term paradigm was seldom used until Joel Barker wrote a book on paradigms, and within a short time, people were having paradigm shifts. I'm amazed at how well we got along without knowing about paradigms. Benchmarking and best practices have become the concepts of the Nineties. What we need to understand is that while all of these activities have value, at some point we need to implement them and go back to work. While some people are in meetings, or out benchmarking, or creating a vision, someone in the plant or the company is making the product that makes the money that allows them to participate in these activities. There's a point where it gets real boring working on the line while other people are out using up the company's resources benchmarking the competition.

There is no fast fix to change. Everybody wants to go to heaven, but nobody wants to die. Everybody wants to be thin, but nobody wants to diet. Everybody wants things to change, but nobody wants to do the difficult things that make change happen. Commitment means being willing to do those difficult things, not just once, but over and over, until they become normal, accepted behavior.

It probably goes without saying, but if change is going to occur, there are some fundamental steps that have to be taken. Words alone won't make it happen. Management working alone will not make it happen. Together, with everyone involved in the cultural transformation, is the only way it will work. Resistance is part of change. Energy wasted resisting change, properly redirected, can become energy for change.

Jay Wilber, *United We Stand*, 1996.

It seems to me that we have a tendency to go from one extreme to another, sometimes throwing the baby out with the bath water. We have a difficult time finding balance, moving from heavy-handed hierarchical management to empowered work forces that, in reality, are not at all empowered. Somewhere between the two there's a happy medium. It seems to me that we need to reevaluate our employee involvement programs and find this common ground. One company I worked with instituted what they called the Ten Square Foot Rule. This meant that anytime a problem arose in the production line, line workers looked within ten square feet to find the solution. In other words, the employees were trusted and empowered and, as a result, their creativity and initiative soared. It might not sound as scientific or as exciting as benchmarking, but over the long haul, it seems to me it's working very well.

It Seems To Me...

To Solve The Problems In Our Communities, We Need To Invite The People That We Perceive As The Problem To The Party.

13. Locking Up The Problem

It seems to me that, in our criminal justice system, we're trying to lock up the problem. A few months ago I was in the state of Virginia where they have over 50 prisons, many constructed over the last few years. Texas, California, Oregon and many other states have been building prisons at an unprecedented rate. I was recently in Eastern Oregon where an institution has been expanded to house 3,000 inmates at a cost of seventy-six million tax dollars. Idaho is now in the process of building a new institution to be managed by a correctional corporation, a somewhat new phenomenon. The increase in the prison populations over the last 10 years is absolutely mind-boggling. The director of a state correctional system recently told me that he now has 14-year old kids who are doing 25-year sentences without parole. Prison populations are getting younger and younger while serving longer and longer sentences. Another significant change has been a dramatic increase in women prisoners. I was recently in the state of Virginia, where they had just completed a new women's prison that will house over 1,500 inmates. There are five or six prisons in California that will each house as many as 4,000 women.

The cost of housing an inmate in a correctional setting varies from state to state, but generally runs between $20,000 and $35,000 per year. The cost for building new prison cells ranges from a low of $40,000 to a high of $80,000, depending on the level of security in a particular institution. We have well over a million men and women locked up in adult correctional institutions. This does not include city and county jails, nor does it include the men and women who are on probation and parole.

We are incarcerating more people on a per capita basis in California than any country in the world other than South Africa or the Soviet Union.
                              Newsweek, August 9, 1982.

When we step back from this massive problem and look at the frenzied drive to lock men and women up, we need to ask ourselves some questions: Is this solving the problem? Are our streets safer?

Can we comfortably walk our city parks at night? Can our children enter safe schools and participate in an environment that is conducive to learning?

We went through some rather bizarre experiences in the Sixties and Seventies. The pendulum had swung far to the side of treatment and rehabilitation. However, during this time, we invested millions and millions of dollars with no research, no follow-up, and no documentation on whether anything was really working. After all this, many so-called experts declared that rehabilitation did not work. It seems to me that, somewhere in all of this madness, our collective psyche determined that behavior can't be changed and that the only solution is to lock up the problem. However, this is a very shortsighted solution. Most of the men and women who are currently locked up in our correctional institutions will return to their communities in a few short years and, unless something happens that interrupts and changes their behavior, they will return to prison again and again at a tremendous cost to society.

I have been involved in the criminal justice system most of my life (the first 20 years was not by choice). I am far from a do-gooder or a knock-kneed liberal. I believe that a criminal act should be punished, and that the punishment should be swift, sure and consistent. I have three children and ten grandchildren and I have a tremendous desire for them to grow up in a safe environment. Swift and sure punishment is not a part of our criminal justice system today. In fact, the criminal justice system has become more of a system of bartering where a criminal act can be excused by agreeing to testify against a co-conspirator or a co-defendant. What's more, the crime may be ten years old by the time the punishment is inflicted. The State of Texas recently executed a 38-year-old man who had committed his crime at the age of 17. Twenty-one years after the crime, they decided to kill him. I say this not to judge, but rather to share an awareness. We are spending tremendous resources on the back end of the problem, while programs that provide intervention or alternative sentencing are struggling for a pittance just to survive. I was with a group of correctional staff recently in a state where they were investing millions of dollars in construction and hardware. And yet, in the same state, the people working to improve the inmate's chances for rehabilitation and release were complaining that they couldn't find $15 for an inmate treatment program.

Somehow, we need to reevaluate our investment on the front end of the problem. How do we keep men and women from becoming consumers of correctional services, and how do we keep men and women who are released from prison from doing life sentences on the installment plan?

I have a philosophy that I would like to share with the reader. If there was a war (God forbid), and an invading army caused us to have to retreat out of our community, it would be wise to have someone plant land mines so that when the invading army entered our community they would be injured by tripping on the mines. When the war is over, and the invading army moves out and we are able to return, an important task will be digging up the land mines. The person best equipped to do this is the person who planted the mines in the first place. My friend, David Lewis, grew up on the streets of East Palo Alto. When we got involved together, David told me that he had planted the mines in East Palo Alto, and knew where the hot spots were. I believe that one of the solutions for our communities is to involve those people who planted the mines; to invite the people that we perceive as the problem to the party. So often, the solution lies within the problem.

I grew up on the streets of Philadelphia. My time as a young man running the streets gave me a great awareness of the minefields that exist for those young men and women who are growing up without families. We need to examine the state of families in our cities. In addition, law enforcement and the criminal justice system, churches, social service programs, corporations, and agencies need to be involved. But we need to reallocate resources so there is adequate funding to provide options for men and women both in our inner cities, and rural areas.

I am currently involved in correctional institutions from Virginia to California. I am also involved in community programs across the country. The approach we have taken in the past will not serve our needs over time. Society needs to reevaluate the use of its tax dollars in this massive drive to simply lock up the problem. Over time, our children will suffer for lack of adequate educational dollars, health care will be impacted, and our communities will find scarce resources to improve their environments. Prisons will always be a necessity, but in this world of creativity, technology and human genius, we should be able to come up with an alternative way to solve this problem.

It Seems To Me...

Our Achilles Heel Lies In Our Unwillingness To Commit To What It Takes To Develop Strong, Honest Relationships Whose Foundations Lie In Trust And Integrity.

14. Relationships

It seems to me that the essence of human interaction is our ability to develop rewarding and productive relationships. Whether at home, at work,
at school, or at the grocery store, we spend much of
our time in communication with one another. We
are ultimately creative beings and can create anything, fix anything, dream anything, imagine anything. Our Achilles heel lies in our unwillingness to
commit to what it takes to develop strong, honest
relationships whose foundations lie in trust and integrity.

Relationships become especially frustrating and
are likely to create a good deal of stress during any
change process. Relationships take a lot of effort
even under ideal circumstances, and when you

throw in the challenges created by change, our relationships become strained. No matter what kind of
change you're talking about, organizational or personal, there will inherently be changes in the relationships of the people involved. It would be un-
reasonable not to expect people to be a bit out of their
comfort zones as a result. The key is to not let those
comfort zone challenges thwart our efforts. When
we recognize the discomfort we are facing as a normal response, and continue to work through it, with
time our comfort zones will expand to include the
new behavior.

At the outset of a love relationship, the excitement and intrigue allows us to bring tremendous
energy and interest to the experience. But after the
initial burst of enthusiasm, and we begin to interact
around common place daily events, the relationship
moves to another stage. For those of us who are involved in marriages and partnerships, we are aware
of the tremendous amount of empathy and understanding that is required. When things are going
well, and there is no conflict, then things flow
smoothly; but as soon as conflict is introduced,
whether it be a financial challenge, a conflict in time,
or a challenge in relation to our priorities, the relationship demands a different level of commitment.
To be in a relationship takes commitment, resiliency,
and a willingness to begin anew as often as necessary. What often hinders a relationship is that in-

stead of being willing to let go, IOU's build up, causing us to react inappropriately or with hostility over seemingly insignificant issues. As a friend of mine likes to say, "The problem is no longer the problem. How you handle the problem becomes the problem."

We need to have the intestinal fortitude to apologize, ask forgiveness and continue to build a solid foundation for the relationship. It takes courage to look honestly at ourselves and not just try fixing the blame on the other person.

There are many elements that go into a relationship; one of the most basic is how we choose to communicate with one another. Our words, facial expressions and body language are constantly flowing back and forth. We give messages to others both intentionally and unintentionally.

Conflict enters the picture when our needs and desires are at cross-purposes with others'. This occurs continuously no matter who we're relating with, whether it's spouses, children, teachers, bosses, or co-workers.

We can choose to learn and grow in our awareness and understanding of mutually rewarding human relations, or we can become stuck in narrow, self-serving beliefs and habits which continually keep us at odds with one another. An important way to a healthy relationship is to be willing to search together to find common ground in those areas. In all successful relationships there is no such thing as win-lose; it's either win-win or lose-lose.

I've been talking about strictly personal relationships, but the same rules apply to relationships in organizations. When extending personal relationships to those between union and management, hourly and salaried employees, or between departments, the challenges are compounded. When a new contract is signed between two parties there is an initial honeymoon period. However, as soon as the first conflict or the first major challenge emerges, we have a tendency to give up on the agreement and go back to the tool we're most comfortable with. Abraham Maslow said, "If the only tool you have is a hammer, then you tend to view every problem as a nail." Some of us use withdrawal as a tool when conflicts arise; others use intimidation. For relationships to work long-term, we need not necessarily like each other and we certainly are not always going to agree with one another, but one essential ingredient is a sense of trust and the tenacity to work through conflicts. Conflicts are a natural part of life. The only people who don't have conflicts are those who are comatose.

Conflicts should be perceived as an opportunity for both parties to learn and to move to another level of awareness and effectiveness. Organizations build planes that will fly across oceans, automobiles that nearly drive themselves, barges that move up and down the rivers, or medicines that keep people alive, yet we are still stuck at the starting gate in terms of sound relationships, both personal and professional. In order for us to move beyond our current state of affairs, we must renew our commitment to healthy relationships. It's refreshing to see an executive and a union leader who are able to recognize each other's responsibilities, disagree on specific points, and still maintain the trust and belief in one another's ability to reach their common goals.

In my experience with inmates, one of the most difficult challenges for men and women coming out of prison settings is to establish healthy relationships. We require advanced degrees of our administrators, and yet don't even question their knowledge of human relations. We are dazzled when young people demonstrate computer skills, but barely acknowledge the child who shows care and concern for his friends. We are masters at developing training materials in technical skills, but we spend little, if any, time working with people to develop tools and techniques for establishing successful relationships. This challenge encompasses almost every aspect of our lives. It relates to parents and children, spouses and partners, union and management, racial groups and nations, and yet we have placed this issue low on our priority list in terms of investment of resources.

It seems to me that we need to go back to square one and begin to revisit our relationships with each other and make a new commitment to working through conflict to develop long-term partnerships.

It Seems To Me...

Today, Even Young Men And Women With The Best Intentions Are At Risk In Certain Communities And Cities.

15. Youth At Risk

It seems to me that the last two decades have been particularly challenging times for the young people in America. The massive changes that have taken place have shaken the foundation that once stabilized our society. Change is a constant in today's world, and security is an illusion. In the past, a young man or woman could follow the same path their parents took and be guaranteed a fairly secure future. A teenager could walk the streets at night without fear of violence. School was a safe haven reserved for learning. Drive-by shootings, drugs and violence didn't exist in most places and where they did, could be easily avoided. Today, a young man or woman with the best intentions is at-risk in certain communities and cities.

The gradual shift in the content of television and music has brought a new awareness to our youth. Positive role models are few and far between in movies, magazines, and our daily fare of television shows. It's a new world and, as adults, we have not done a good job of helping young people manage their changing environments. Drugs, alcohol and violence have become daily occurrences even in the best schools. Teenage pregnancy has become a common challenge for today's young people as well as their parents.

In my travels across the United States, I find more and more people who are willing to throw in the towel on today's youth. Juvenile crime is on the rise and more and more states are reducing the age at which we lock young men and women up in maximum security prisons where they learn to become professional criminals. The role models portrayed by some of our athletes, some of our political leaders, and some of our military leaders, are certainly not consistent with the values of the past. Fear, driven by the media, pervades society. A violent crime committed in Arkansas, California, or the hill country of Kentucky is played in living rooms from Virginia to Montana. The act is not only shown on the five o'clock news, it is shown again and again, only to become a movie or a best selling book.

Caught up in this bizarre set of circumstances, young people can become disillusioned and seek comfort in dangerous places. We, as taxpayers, are willing to invest billions of dollars on the back end of the system by building prisons to deal with the adult criminal. And while these billions of dollars are being invested in prisons, our communities lack resources for young people to have an outlet for the creativity and needs that are so paramount in their minds.

> *There is no sadder sight than a young pessimist.*
> Mark Twain

I go into inner cities where parks have deteriorated and have become unsafe for the community's youth. Community centers fight for dollars to keep their doors open and educational institutions are forced to use outdated books and materials. However, in the midst of this seemingly impossible challenge, there are rays of hope. Deschutes County in Central Oregon has begun a process to redirect its attention to the front end of the system. To house a young man or woman in a state correctional facility in Oregon costs approximately $46,000 annually. Denny Maloney, Deschutes County's Director of Corrections, has received legislative approval that will transfer the $46,000 for each young person who would otherwise be sent to a state institution, directly to his county. The county can then use that money for intervention, prevention, and rehabilitation services. If they can't deal with a particular child at the county level, then they must send the young person, along with the $46,000, to the state. This simple paradigm shift puts the resources at the

root of the problem. It provides the resources necessary to impact the young people's behavior in their
community through alternative sentencing and di-
versionary tactics such as drug treatment, family
counseling, and employment skills training.

Not only have they diverted the resources back
to the community, the county has also passed a bond
measure and built a juvenile justice center that offers a wide range of programs and opportunities to
work with youth. Part of the facility is a lock-up
facility. But the intent of lock-up is to stop the young
person long enough to interrupt their behavior, provide some new tools, and move them back into interaction with their family and community. If they
exhaust their community resources, the state correctional facility still looms large across the mountains.

Jerry Andres, CEO of Eagle Crest Group, one of
the major employers in Deschutes County, is a good
example of how one person committed to his community can make a difference. Jerry has established
a strong mentoring program for high school students
who are at-risk. Most of the managers of Eagle Crest
get involved with this mentoring project. There
have been many exciting success stories that have
developed from this effort.

The county has also mobilized agencies and
non-profit organizations to participate in the solution. Annette Bessey, Director of Operations of Op-

portunities Unlimited, Inc., a non-profit organization which was started to address the issues of the at-risk youth population, has been heavily involved in this project. Annette, a former consumer of correctional services in the state of Oregon, has turned her life around and is intent on giving back at the community level. Again, it's a matter of recruiting the people who planted the mines. Those people have a driving desire to reach out to young people.

Leaders need to have the courage to involve people that have heretofore been excluded if we are going to bring about constructive change in our communities. Our young people need and deserve the support of everyone in their communities — people in education, health, law enforcement, business, churches, and above all, their parents.

Part Three
Lessons Learned...

Lessons Learned...

Learning Through Self-Discovery Leads To True Accountability For The Choices We Make.

16. Change Is An Inside Job

The idea that change is an inside job has to do with the fact that each of us is accountable for our own life. However, it goes beyond the individual and surfaces as one of the common challenges we face. That is, we are always trying to change other people! People run around claiming they've changed people's lives. The fact is, you can provide people with support and new tools, but change is still an inside job. Or, we keep waiting for others to initiate the changes that we feel are necessary. We can provide an environment where change is encouraged and we can establish support systems that help sustain the change, but in the final analysis, making change is a matter of personal choice.

Years ago, I learned that, as we mature and develop our outlook on life, we become more and more resistant to any information or data that suggests we may need to change. We are always trying to keep things together in our brain, so when we receive information that conflicts with our outlook or opinion, we have a tendency to reject it out of hand or, at a minimum, strongly resist it. I'm sure this isn't true of you, the reader, but it seems true for most people.

Only fools and dead men don't change their minds. Fools won't. Dead men can't.
John H. Patterson/American Manufacturer

When we are offered new information about change or a new approach to improving relationships, our first thought is often to identify those people who really need it. "Boy, I wish my wife or my husband were here. She/he really needs to hear this." If I'm speaking to a corporation I hear, "Where the hell is management?" Or, "Where the hell is the union?" It's always someone else. What we're really saying in this situation is, "I'm okay the way that I am. If I could just get those other people to change, things would be great!" This becomes one of the primary barriers to changing a culture.

Adult learning is a process of self-discovery. When we connect with something we read or hear that allows us to discover alternative solutions, we take ownership of the information. When we take part in an interactive learning experience, we have the opportunity to experience the self-discovery process that leads to true accountability for the choices we make.

I have come to feel that the only learning which significantly influences behavior is self-discovered, self-appropriated learning.
Carl Rogers, *On Becoming a Person*, 1961.

Many times the learning process is really a process of rediscovering something that has been buried through lack of use. A couple of years ago I was teaching a session at a shipyard in Louisville, Kentucky. The participants were laborers who work in a very tough environment. There was a big ol' dude named Slim who was sitting in the back row. Slim had been working there for 30 years. His arms were folded across his chest and I was sure he would rather be out in the shipyard. I told about a session I had with another group and how I had suggested at the end of that day's training that they do something nice for someone that evening. When we got back together the next morning, one of the men who'd been there the previous day came up to me and jokingly said, "Man, you got me in trouble last night." I asked, "How so?" He said, "On my way home I bought my wife a bouquet of flowers. When I gave them to her, she got upset. She asked, 'Why are you giving me these flowers? What have you been up to?'" We had a good laugh, but I thought how sad it is that we develop relationships where doing something nice for someone is suspect. I shared this example with the shipyard group to illustrate a point. The next day, the big rough guy, Slim, approached me and I could see that something had happened. He took me aside and said, "You really touched me yesterday. I worked overtime after the session and when I got home my wife was already in bed. I went in and woke her up and told her how much I loved her and how much she meant to me." Slim continued, "My wife started to cry." Now, if someone had told Slim, "You should go home and tell your wife how much you love her," there would have been a major conflict! But because he was allowed to learn through a process of self-discovery, Slim was able to accept the information and apply it in his life.

In a follow-up session a couple of months later with the same shipyard employees, I asked how often people gave positive feedback to those who are important in their lives. Slim spoke up and said, "I hadn't done it for years, but I've done it every day since you were here." Change is an inside job, but we need to offer new tools in a non-threatening way that allows people to discover the areas in their life that have become traps and barriers to personal growth.

Most people want the same things out of life. They want to be treated with dignity and respect. They want to be involved. They want to be fairly compensated. They want equal access to opportunities. They want to feel that what they do makes a difference. What they don't want is to have someone trying to cram change down their throat. They don't want someone else determining what's good for them. They don't want some consultant or government agency coming in and dictating how they should function and do their job.

People need to see the pay value (the "what's in it for me") to take an active role in a training process. If the goal is just to improve the company's bottom line, or to satisfy some bureaucratic machinery, then it will be difficult to get active involvement. The process of self-discovery works because, unlike other processes that imply there's something wrong with people, that they need to be "fixed," it offers a participant the opportunity for self-determination. They make the decision to change and, equally important, they decide what that change will be.

Prisons have designed programs that are like car washes. The assumption is that the inmate will go through the program and will come out looking like the picture we've created of what they *should* look like. The inmate's reaction is "Yeah, right. I'll participate in your program because I want out, but you ain't changing me." Programs come and programs go, but the inmate continues to repeat the same old behavior. The programs have usually been designed by psychologists or therapists. The concepts and principles are generally sound, but they are presented in a manner that resembles manipulation and creates resistance.

Most of the thousands of inmates that I've worked with over the past twenty-five years that have made long-term changes in their lives did so through a process of self-discovery. Self-discovery creates ownership and ownership facilitates internal change. The concepts and techniques that I've used to change my life from a dishonest convict to an honest citizen are written in books and were probably stressed by psychologists and counselors during my years in prison. But, until I discovered them myself, they didn't have any real impact on me. The old adage that "you can lead a horse to water but you can't make him drink," unfortunately, holds a lot of truth. We need to provide new information in a non-threatening way that facilitates the self-discovery process. We need to create cultures that support changes in the way we interact and communicate. We need to develop trust that people will do the right thing and allow input from even the most cantankerous employees. "Change is an inside job," but it *can* be facilitated and the best way is through self-discovery.

Lessons Learned...

The Greatest Lesson In Life Is That We All Have The Power To Control How We Respond To External Circumstances.

17. Who Said Life Was Fair?

We live in an imperfect world and life isn't always fair. The good guy doesn't always get the girl, and justice is not always blind. But one lesson I've learned that has served me well over the years is that I can control how I respond to life's inequities.

There was a long period in my life when I cursed and railed over the injustice perpetrated on human kind. I fixed the blame on the government, law enforcement, the guards in prison, or just "they and them" out there who, I perceived, were purposely messing up my life. I had no control over my life, because it was the damn system that kept me from being successful. Or so I thought.

Man must cease attributing his problems to his environment, and learn again to exercise his will, his personal responsibility, in the realm of faith and morals.
                                        Albert Schweitzer

At that time in my life, everyone seemed to feel just like I did. I walked the yard with the other prisoners and we would bitch and complain about how unfair the system was. "It's okay for the politicians to steal, but they lock you and me up for five lousy bucks," or "Sh— man, I'm doing five years for having an ounce of dope, and it wasn't even mine." "Prisons are big business man, they gotta keep 'em full." "They set me up! Hell, I had myself a little job and me and my old lady had a nice place and they came in and busted me for having a shotgun. They claim I robbed some drugstore. Hell, man, I didn't even know the gun was in my house. Now, here I am doing six damn years. It just ain't fair. Sh—, man, when I get out I'm going to . . ." and the mind continues to go round and round, weaving a web of powerlessness. We were locked up behind the walls. In prison, the normal responses to our current situation were, "It's not my fault," and "They did it to me." However, when you get out, this mindset is so ingrained, you carry it with you out into the merciless world that, you believe, is set up to cause you to fail.

I had been out of prison for a while, fighting the

battle of survival in a system that, I thought, was out to get me, when I participated in a seminar that shocked my senses. Something happened to me that changed my life. There was a paradigm shift inside of my being, and I broke free. The most profound realization occurred — that I was accountable, that I could choose how I responded to what happened in my life. It was as though I'd been sitting in the dark, and someone turned on the lights. The first step to change is an awareness, and I was now aware that I was the problem as well as the solution.

This is not to say that life is always fair. It isn't. And there are circumstances outside ourselves that impact our lives. There are times when the justice system is not just, and government is corrupt. All of these things are true, but the realization that I have the power to control how I respond to these external circumstances was one of the greatest lessons I learned.

Today, after all these years, I am still amazed at how many people are trapped in the "it's not my fault" or the "that's just the way it is" syndrome. When I conduct a training program for companies or corporations, the conversations take me back to the big yard in Walla Walla.

"It's the damn management; they don't know what the hell they're doing." "The union just won't get on board. They're going to bankrupt the company." "Sh—-, it's the foreign competition. How the hell are we supposed to compete against their labor costs?" "It's the engineers." "No, it's the damn Generation X employees. They just don't want to work." "The government regulations are the problem. OSHA's out to close us down." Or, it's the weather, and finally it's almost always, "they and them out there." Who are they?

There are certainly factors and circumstances outside ourselves that have an impact on how our lives work. Sometimes management is a pain in the ass and sometimes the union is. Sometimes the economy or government regulations can make life difficult. But how we respond to these circumstances makes all the difference in how effective we are and how we feel about our lives.

Feeling out of control causes us to wait for somebody out there to do something. "Why don't 'they' fix the problem!" "I wouldn't be on welfare if 'they' would just get me a decent job." "This community wouldn't be so dangerous if the cops would just do their jobs." "If 'they' would just keep 'those' people out of our neighborhood we wouldn't have these problems." "If 'they' would just give us the money, things would be fine." "If 'they'd' just get a program for me, I'd stay off drugs." "It's not my fault."

We live in an imperfect world with imperfect people. Justice is not always blind and the good guy doesn't always get the girl. But, one of the most important lessons life has taught me is that I am accountable. If I don't like the way things are working, then I need to ask myself, "What can I do about it?" Sometimes the answer is that there's *nothing* I can do to change a situation, but I can always change the way I respond to it.

God grant me the Serenity
To accept the things I cannot change,
The Courage to change the things I can,
And the Wisdom to know the difference.

Lessons Learned...

For A Change Initiative To Bring Long-Term Results, It Must Be Driven Into The Culture Deeply Enough To Enable It To Sustain Itself Through Leadership Change.

18. Transcending Leadership

The process of change needs to be able to transcend leadership.

Many of the change initiatives that are implemented in institutions, corporations or agencies are unable to sustain themselves through a change in leadership. When an executive or union leader endorses a change initiative, it will stay alive as long as they support the process. If the executive moves to another plant or department, the initiative generally dies. If a union leader retires or is defeated in an election, the initiative generally falls with him or her. For a change initiative to bring long-term results, it needs to be driven into the culture deep

enough to enable it to sustain itself through leadership change.

When I first began to work with the Department
of Corrections in the State of Oregon, they had a director who was a visionary and believed it was possible to empower people and transfer responsibility
to employees. He also believed that you could manage society's criminal justice problems without
building more prisons. Oregon was an exciting
model that I was able to use across the United States
as an example. Many of the wardens and managers
within the Oregon system took ownership of the initiatives that Frank Hall, the Director in Oregon, had
instituted. When Oregon went through a change in
Governors, Frank Hall was replaced and, although
the state of Oregon has begun to build more prison
cells, many of the initiatives started by the former
Director are still alive and well. They were driven
deeply enough into the culture that they could sustain themselves through the leadership change.

This is not always true in industrial plants or
government agencies. A plant manager can initiate
a program and as soon as he or she is transferred
the program is put on the shelves. A union leader
that supports a change initiative program can find
themselves faced with a political challenge. In fact,
the change initiative has even been used as an issue
to defeat the incumbent. As a result, people in the
organization become even more disillusioned and

hesitate to support any future initiatives.

Military installations, even those that have a large civilian work force, are generally headed by a military leader. That leader usually has a short tour of duty, and the civilian management knows that the leader will be gone within the next two years. So when change is initiated, they simply "hunker down" and give lip service to the change, knowing that it won't last. The Merck Pharmaceutical plant at Rahway, New Jersey, where I've been involved for the past six years, has kept the change initiatives alive in spite of a turnover of plant managers. Guy Fleming has been the President of the OCAW since I first became involved with Merck. Because of his support, Merck has successfully kept the "Framework for Change" process alive. His honest approach to the membership has allowed him to win reelection twice since the initiative started. John Mathis, a labor relations representative, has also supported the process over the years. Guy and John have their share of conflicts, but they don't let the conflicts affect the "Framework" process. There have been three plant managers at the Rahway plant since my involvement, and each one has been willing to support the change initiative.

Developing champions throughout the organization drives the change initiative deep enough into the culture that it can take on a life of its own. The follow-through and commitment by leadership is essential for this to occur. When you're dealing with an organized workforce, it's important that union leadership has enough time to demonstrate to the membership that what they're doing will bring value to their lives. It's also important that management understand that the union's position is to represent their members' interests.

At the government level, we pass laws and legislation that allows certain practices to sustain themselves through a change of political leadership. But unless the political leader supports the legislation, it will find itself mired in bureaucratic paperwork.

Most corporations have a tendency to train the leadership teams under the premise that they will set the tone and everyone will follow right along. That's good in theory, but if the culture you're dealing with is toxic, it will be necessary to bring the negativity to the surface and deal with it before you can move forward.

It takes time to initiate cultural change. It also takes leadership support, both in terms of time and resources. Companies and organizations waste millions of dollars by implementing programs that are not supported by the employees. It's important that a cross-section of people in an organization be involved in the planning stages prior to implementing a change initiative. Constant communication of the ideas will insure that the employees will see the long-term value for them. In order for long-term change to become a reality, employees need to take ownership of the process at all levels of an organization. When this occurs, the initiative will survive leadership change.

Lessons Learned...

If You Want To Be Loved, Love. If You Want To Be Respected, Respect.

19. Life Is A Reciprocal Process

You get back from life what you put into it. This has become an important principle in my life. The challenge with this concept is that it usually takes time to realize a return on your investment.

Results take time to measure. When you plant a flower seed or an acorn, it doesn't sprout overnight. In fact, the acorn will take years to grow into an oak tree. The flower takes less time, but still doesn't blossom in the first few weeks. Both the acorn and the flower will grow faster and will be healthier when nurtured by the person responsible for planting the seed. We do this quite well with our children. We support, remind and nurture the child until the seed is well-grounded. However, we fail in this process when we're dealing with adults.

Creating a healthier, more productive life is much the same process as planting seeds. Those of us who are parents can certainly attest to the truth of this process when raising children. The nurturing and consistency of love, discipline and feedback can take years to finally show returns. For example, there have been times when I felt that my children would never become independent, productive adults, but at last I can look back and say, "Damn, they've arrived;" sometimes in spite of me, I'm afraid.

Establishing my trustworthiness, both for myself and others, took time. For some of us it may be a case of reestablishing trust, but for me it was something I'd never had. When I made the changes in my own life, it didn't automatically change other peoples' opinions of me. Law enforcement, correctional officers, other inmates and people in the community knew me. They knew that I'd run games before, and in their minds this was just another game. I understood this, and it caused me to be more aware of my environment because I knew that if something illegal happened and I was in the neighborhood, I was history. I couldn't blame anyone but myself. I'd created a reputation as a thief and manipulator, and therefore it was my responsibility to change it. I set out on a mission to establish trust. If I made a promise or commitment I would follow through regardless of the circumstances. I always tried to give more than was expected of me. I made a conscious choice to tell the truth even when it would have been easier to keep quiet. Before too long, I began to experience a change in peoples' reactions to me. People who had known me in the past were offering me opportunities and support. The first people to accept the new Gordon Graham were the convicts who'd grown up with me. They knew I was real. But correctional officers who had known the other side of me took more convincing. It was a slow process, but gradually my reputation began to change. Wardens were inviting me to speak to inmates and staff. The reciprocal process was taking place. Most importantly, all of these changes must be done with an honest spirit, or it's just another form of manipulation.

If you want to be loved, you need to give love to others. If you want respect, then you need to respect others. If you want people to contribute to a project or goal, then you need to contribute. Sometimes we need to be willing to reach out even if we may be rejected. So often relationships break down in a marriage, or in a business, and neither party is willing to reach out. "I'm not talking to them until they talk to me first," or "I'll trust them when they are trustworthy." You get back what you put in. Life is a reciprocal process.

I have a close friend in East Palo Alto, California, a city that had the unsavory distinction of being named the murder capital of the country in 1991. My friend, David Lewis, is an ex-convict, a former Black Guerilla Gang leader and a recovering addict. David, like myself, reclaimed his life through a process of self-discovery. The past seven years he has worked endless hours giving back to his community. David works with men and women who have AIDS, and he has founded a non-profit organization called Free at Last. Through David, the mayor, and other community activists, violence in East Palo Alto has been reduced by 86%.

David Lewis has given back not only to the community of East Palo Alto, but to prisons up and down the state of California, modeling the idea that change is possible. The reciprocal process has brought David many rewards. Besides being awarded the California Peace Prize in 1995 for his efforts to reduce inner city violence, he has gained national attention, and is included as a member of a national foundation's board of directors. He is a guest lecturer at colleges and universities, and is trusted by police, business owners, government leaders, citizens, and ex-offenders in his community.

Man did not weave the web of life, he is merely a strand in it. Whatever he does to the web, he does to himself.

American Chief Seattle

David doesn't make a lot of money; he doesn't live in a big house or drive a Mercedes. He does what he does because of his commitment to his community. We all need to make money, but it's the spirit of why we do what we do that really counts. You can't buy the kind of rewards that David gets when he visits a home for recovering mothers and children in his community. We're talking about people's lives.

If you cut an apple in half and open the apple up, anyone can count the number of seeds in the apple. But, no one can count the number of apples in a seed. So we plant seeds. We can't guarantee that every seed will sprout, and we can't always control when they'll sprout. The important thing is to just keep planting.

Someone planted a seed in my brain 27 years ago, and the ground was fertile. It was nurtured by my wife, my children, and a group of friends. I've had the privilege of planting seeds in the minds of people like David Lewis, and David Lewis, like many others, plants seeds in his community.

You get out of life what you put into it. You need to be actively involved in those things that are important to you. You need to get out of bed and get "in the game." We need to have the tenacity and courage to handle setbacks and to keep our goals in mind. At the same time, we need to enjoy the excitement and the challenge of the journey itself, because results take time to measure.

Lessons Learned...

We Have To Believe
That Any One Of
Us Can Make A
Difference And
That We Have
Access To A Power
Much Greater Than
Ourselves.

20. God Didn't Make No Junk

This lesson is difficult for some of us to internalize. It sounds like a nice little saying that should be true, but for years I thought maybe I was an exception to the rule. God, Allah, Jehovah, whatever your higher being is called "didn't make no junk." "Birth equals worth." This was not something that I came to understand easily. In the material world where worth is often measured by money, possessions, degrees or appearance, it's not unusual for us to sometimes feel like junk. *God didn't make no junk.* When we get caught up in circumstances that seem to be unfair, it's easy to feel as though God plays favorites. "How come I can't get a damn break?" If there is a God, He/She sure as hell isn't on the job or I wouldn't be in this mess."

I grew up in a world devoid of any form of spiritual teaching. Religion was not a part of my early life. Oh, I knew there was supposed to be a God that acted as a kind of overseer of people on earth, but that was the extent of my awareness. Then, as I grew into adulthood and began my career as a safecracker and convict, it served me better not to spend time thinking about the God stuff, 'cause He sure as hell wouldn't have approved of my lifestyle. So I practiced the out-of-sight, out-of-mind routine. I just tried not to think about it too much. Then, in prison, it seemed like the convicts who went to religious services were the snitches and the weaker guys, so it wasn't a place I frequented.

I read a lot in prison, so naturally I learned about the various religions. I learned that there were a hell of a lot of different beliefs about God and how you were supposed to live to be accepted into Heaven, which sounded pretty darn good to a convict. I mean, who wouldn't want a piece of *that* rock? When I was doing a year in the hole, completely isolated, the only book I was allowed to read was the Bible. So I read the Bible to pass the time. I was looking for the exciting parts; the parts with sex and things that made sense to me.

During that year of solitary confinement, I also tried to talk God into getting me out of the damn

Hole. But, that wasn't in the grand scheme of things and when I got out, I put the God stuff on the back burner and got on with my life.

Years later, when I had been released from prison and had turned my life around and things seemed to be moving in the right direction, I still felt a sense of emptiness — that I wasn't quite okay. I was involved in teaching self-image psychology across the country, but sometimes I felt like an imposter. "What if people find out who I really am and how I feel?" I thought. At the time, I didn't link any of these feelings to God or spirituality, although I knew it was an area that I needed to address.

I had a wife and children by then and I knew it was important that my kids develop a solid foundation for life. So we started taking them to church. It just so happened that my mentor was Catholic, so we participated in the Catholic Church. Going to church was just an intellectual exercise for me. I felt no real connection to the rituals, but I endured for my children's sake. I didn't resonate to the crackers and wine, and I felt awkward and out of place.

Nonetheless, I had grown in my awareness of the world and had become quite good at delivering the seminar on self-image psychology. I was presenting programs to government agencies and businesses in cities across the country. I was also spending a good portion of my time working with inmates in prisons. By now I was consciously asking God to come into my life and flow through me and touch the hearts of the people in my seminars. I was living my life with the idea that there is a reason for my existence and that we are all created equal under God and that birth equals worth. Instead of looking outside myself for confirmation, I looked inward and communicated my desire to be all that I can be to the Supreme Being. I no longer felt as though I was inferior. I knew that many people were smarter than me, had more possessions than me, were prettier than me, but I felt okay with me. I'd filled the empty spot that had been nagging at my being for so many years. But, for some reason, that hasn't been enough for some people! I'm honest, I treat people with respect, I think I'm a decent father, a good partner, and I try to contribute in a positive way to the world I live in. But, it seems that some people aren't okay with that. I have been asked so many times over the years, "Are you a Christian?" How do you respond to that? Because when people ask that question, what they are really saying is, "If you don't believe as I do, you ain't okay." So I tap dance around the question and try to avoid an argument, or worse still, a lecture on how I should believe. I have friends who are Muslim, Jewish, Catholic, Buddhist, Mormon, Seventh Day Adventist, Protestant, Baptist, Hindu, Lutheran, Methodist, and I'm okay with that!

There is no meaning to life except the meaning man

gives his life by the unfolding of his powers.
                                        Erich Fromm

How do you live your life? Are you fair? Do you treat all people with dignity? Are you honest; do you keep your word? Do you contribute to your community? Those are the more important issues. I believe when the final tally is taken, God will be okay with your brand of religion if you've lived a decent existence on earth. Hopefully, God can get over the first half of my life, or I'm in a world of hurt!

We limit ourselves by not accepting that we are all born equal and that we have the right to play in life's game in whatever way we choose. If we are honest and do things for the right reasons, there are no limits to what we can accomplish. But, if our self-worth comes from anything external, then we are in big trouble. I struggled with that lesson before I finally accepted and internalized the reality that "God didn't make no junk." We have to believe in ourselves and believe that we can make a difference and that we have access to a power much greater than ourselves.

Lessons Learned...

Dignity And
Respect Are
Non-Negotiable
In Any
Relationship Or
Organization.

21. Dignity And Respect Are Non-Negotiable

Each of us has the right to be treated with dignity and respect. This is not a negotiable item, yet in many situations, we allow people to treat us disrespectfully. People in positions of authority often use their power in ways that take away the self-esteem of the people working with them. Often when we find ourselves in conflict with others, we resort to practices that strip away the self-respect of the individual with whom we have conflict.

I was recently involved with a police department that was doing some work with youth. The thing that struck me was the lack of respect on both sides. Somehow, over time, the young people had lost their regard for law enforcement, and law enforcement seemed to have no respect for the young person's point of view. You can disagree with people's opinions and still respect their right to express themselves.

A recent survey conducted with teenagers in an upper middle class community in the western part of the United States provided some interesting feedback. The young people were bothered by the fact that adults would not look at them when they passed on the sidewalk. They said that the adults looked down or looked away, and from the teenager's point of view, this was a nonverbal expression of a lack of respect. This may or may not be the truth from the adult's point of view, but that's the way the message was received by the young people.

When you fail to respect the opinions of employees, this sends a signal that they don't count. Most companies say their employees are their most valuable asset and yet when we don't treat them that way it becomes nothing more than lip service. We say our children are our number one priority in the country and yet child abuse and neglect are at an all-time high. And those of us who aren't doing the abusing are usually the ones who are looking the other way. When I talk to people in organizations about treating people with honesty and dignity and respect, someone will inevitably say, "Well, that's just common sense!" And I'll say, "You're right, it is! Unfortunately, it's not common *practice*!"

Sometimes we disrespect people's feedback because they don't have a degree, or they don't dress like us, or look like us. Daniel Goldman's book, *Emotional Intelligence*, talks about a form of intelligence that cannot be measured by I.Q. tests. It's the kind of intelligence that a line staff employee has, or that a person who grows up on the streets develops. In order to tap into this intelligence, and we could all benefit from doing that, it's necessary to respect the other person and his or her experience.

It's amazing to me that we have finally decided to ask the people who are doing the jobs in our companies how to improve the processes they're involved with. So often we ignore the talents and creativity of people because they are "only" a machinist or "only" a truck driver. When you treat people with dignity and respect, it's amazing how much they have to offer and how willing they are to contribute.

People Rule #9: Dehumiliate. Eliminate policies and practices, almost always tiny, of the organization which demean and belittle human dignity. Rid yourself - immediately - of obvious insults such as executive parking spaces. Eliminate ten 'demeaners' every sixty days.
Tom Peters, *A Passion for Excellence.*

Even in a prison environment, people need to be treated with dignity and respect. You can be hard-nosed and strict, but if you treat people with dignity, you will get the same in return. I have learned that the best way to achieve a win/win situation is to respect people's right to be who they are and to honor everyone's viewpoint.

Dignity and respect are also the foundation for healthy family relationships. I have had the opportunity to raise three children, and my willingness to respect their individuality and treat them with respect, even though I often disagreed with their behavior, has allowed us to become good friends as adults. It's amazing to me how easy it is to lose this awareness, in industrial plants, government agencies and in organizations. When people feel disrespected and lose their dignity, they withdraw and the result is a decrease in the bottom line performance.

Dignity and respect should be a given. Treating people any other way is not okay.

Lessons Learned...

Resiliency,
The Willingness
To Work Through
Conflicts And
Setbacks,
Is Essential To
Any Long-Term
Success.

22. Resiliency

Resiliency is the ability to bounce back from set-backs and to work through conflicts and challenges without giving up.

Resiliency can be learned. Some people seem to be born with a natural ability to handle setbacks without giving up. They bounce back from rejections or losses with a minimal amount of effort. For others, recovering from setbacks or losses can be close to impossible. Over the years that I've practiced the concepts and techniques, I've learned to take all setbacks as temporary. I wasn't born with this ability, nor did I learn it by osmosis. It was by deliberate intent. Taking the concepts and techniques of affirmations and visualization, I gradually and incrementally internalized the resiliency that allows me to handle rejection, losses, or disappointments with a minimal amount of down-time.

In the past, when I was released from prison and reentered society with a desire to stay out, the first setback, the first time that I got rejected for a job, or the first time that I faced a financial problem, I would revert back to my old behavior. Resiliency, perseverance, the willingness to work through conflicts and setbacks, is essential to any long-term success. We need to become tenacious in our approach to the future. This does not mean that we should lock on to an end result and become unable to change or to redirect our course when it's necessary. But the ability to work through conflict and to handle all setbacks as temporary is a quality that individuals and organizations need to develop. Union and management sign a contract and, within three months, they've allowed conflict or disappointment to cause them to go back to old behaviors. An athlete who cannot handle setbacks has little chance of being successful.

Resiliency is an essential quality in a marriage or any relationship. Marriages always present the partners with opportunities to manage disappointment and setbacks. Without resiliency, the relationships have a real short life span.

One of the qualities of resiliency is the ability to keep your eye on the prize; to see the end result as you would like it to be and recognize that to achieve that end result there are many small, often mundane details that need to be managed. If you focus on the mundane, then setbacks will take on more and more power. But by focusing on the end result, you can manage setbacks and still keep your long-term goal in mind.

Courage is not how a man stands or falls, but how he gets back up again.
John L. Lewis/United Mine Workers
Union President

When I first started this journey, I knew it would require resiliency. I learned a technique that I've used over and over for the past twenty-five years. It's called the flick back, flick up technique. This technique has two aspects to it. When you get caught in a downward spiral, or when things don't seem to be going as well as they should, you can separate yourself from the business of your day, quiet your mind, and flick back to a time when you were faced with similar challenges. Then, flick up to the present and affirm to yourself, "I got through that, and I can get through this." When we're caught up in the situation, it's hard for us to see ourselves moving past the problem to get to the solution. I've used this technique by flicking back to the time when I was in prison on bread and water. I would see myself in that situation, and then flick up to the present, and I would say to myself, "I was strong enough to get through that and I can get through this." It builds my ability to be tenacious and manage setbacks. Another way to use this technique is to flick back to a time when things were going really well, feel the emotion that went with that time, and then bring that emotion up to the current situation. That way, you bring the positive energy and emotion from a previous experience into the current situation. As you practice these techniques, you gradually and incrementally become more and more able to work through setbacks.

I developed tenacity through practice, and it is a quality that has served me well over time. If we are disappointed in a love relationship, we have two choices — never to fall in love again, or to recognize that life is a long-term event and try again. The ability to see setbacks as temporary is a tremendous tool for building resiliency.

When you get to the end of your rope, tie a knot and hang on.
                    Franklin D. Roosevelt

Vince Lombardi once said, "I've never lost a game; I've just run out of time." When you see great athletes who can keep their focus when faced with a lopsided score and still believe they can win, it's a tremendous inspiration to all of us. Often, the company that becomes successful is the one whose leadership just simply refuses to give up.

When I am in a prison working with inmates or

staff, I always remind them that programs come and programs go, that they peak and they fade out. But I'm still here. Our programs are still alive and providing people with new tools. Over the years there have been many times when I've been knocked down, had tough financial challenges or been rejected by correctional leadership and was able to bounce back and come at it from a different direction. If there is one quality that men and women coming out of prison need to internalize it's resiliency, because you will get rejected, you will get knocked down, you will be disappointed, but if you have staying power, you will achieve tremendous long-term happiness.

Resiliency is the key.

Lessons Learned...

You Move Towards And Become Like That Which You Think About Most Of The Time.

23. Self-Talk

Some of the lessons I've learned had an instantaneous impact on my approach to life. Other lessons had to be tested and applied over a period of time before their benefits were realized.

The awareness and understanding of the self-talk concept caused an immediate shift in the way I talked to myself. Self-talk is the constant stream of conversation we carry on with ourselves inside our head as we go through the day. When someone else is talking, we are interpreting what's being said through our own self-talk. When we witness an event, we record our interpretation of it through our self-talk.

This concept really hit me. I could think back on my life and see how I had let my self-talk control me. People would give me information that should have been helpful, but I would negate its value by saying to myself, "That just doesn't work for someone like me, " or "How the hell do you know what it's like to grow up on the streets?" So the good advice had no impact on my attitude or beliefs. I'd let people predict my future by reinforcing a negative self-image. "You'll be in and out of prison for the rest of your life," or "You won't be out six months and you'll be back." Instead of refusing to accept this kind of information, my self-talk would run wild and I'd begin to focus on failure. Since you move toward and become like that which you think about, by focusing on failure long enough, that was exactly what I got.

You get what you expect out of life, not what you want. Many years ago I produced a video series titled, "How To Do Life on the Streets!" The title came from conversations among inmates on prison yards. Walla Walla is the end of the line for inmates in Washington State. It's the maximum security prison, so if you stay in the system long enough, you will eventually wind up in Walla Walla. Inmates who end up in Walla Walla have generally been together in other prisons prior to their arrival there. When a new inmate hits the yard and runs into two or three old friends, the conversation will go something like this: "Hey Gordy, how you doin'? How long were you out?" I would tell them, "I was only out six months man, but they set me up." One of the other inmates would say, "Hell I was out a year!" and the next, "I was out three years!" The self-talk in prison yards sounds like outside is temporary and inside is forever!

Our self-talk is a constant stream of affirmations, or statements of our interpretation of fact. Once I became aware that what I was saying to myself impacted how I lived my life, I learned to redirect my self-talk.

Quite often, we're not even aware of our self-talk. A friend of mine told me about a time when she became aware that she was holding herself back with her own self-talk. She owned her own business and worked long hours and, to keep herself going, she listened to a lot of motivational tapes. One day she was thinking to herself that she really wasn't seeing any results, when she suddenly became aware of the self-talk going on in her head. In the back of her mind, she was telling herself, "Things like this don't work for people like me." By becoming aware of her self-talk, she also became aware that she was carrying around a belief about her ability to achieve her goals.

Once you have this new awareness, you can learn to control your self-talk and change the direction of your life. In our training, we teach people to use affirmations to help them change their self-talk. It may sound strange to you at first, but it works.

The fact is, you're using affirmations all the time. When your self-talk is saying, "This stuff won't work", that's an affirmation. If you tell yourself, "I'm going to be dead tired tomorrow", that's an affirmation. Doesn't it make sense to use affirmations that will help you get a result you'd rather have? It's always been interesting to me that we really admire an athlete who pumps himself up to score the winning touchdown or hit the game-winning homerun yet, when we talk about using affirmations to reach a sales goal or pass a test or get out of prison, we raise our eyebrows and roll our eyes. It's the same thing! Ask anyone who knows me and they'll tell you that when somebody says, "How are you?" to me, my response is always, "Awesome!" and, most days, that's exactly how I feel.

People who are negative and people who are cynics can take the heart out of others. I've become very careful of who I listen to and who I allow to influence me. Or, if I find I'm giving myself negative feedback, I interrupt it and redirect my self-talk to a positive tone. I can't change other people, but I can prevent what they say and do from impacting how I live my life. If you change the way you think, you will change the way you act. A simple, but profound, lesson learned.

A facilitator who works with at-risk youth in Cedar Rapids, Iowa uses an exercise on self-talk where he has young people think about all of the negative affirmations, self-talk statements, that they hear every day. The group then shares those statements and they are recorded on flipcharts. The negative statements that the young people come up with usually fills three or four pieces of flipchart paper. Then they record all of the positive affirmations, self-talk statements, they hear on a daily basis. Sometimes it takes a long time to record even two or three positive statements. That's a sad commentary on our work with youth.

We get used to so much negativity that it becomes difficult to accept the positives about ourselves. Find ways to put positive weights on your children's attitudinal balance scales. Find honest ways to feel good about yourself. Don't let other people take away your heart. Be the best "you" that you can be and recognize that thoughts have power. Self talk is the place to take control.

Lessons Learned...

When We Trust
Ourselves
And Develop
Consistency
Within Ourselves,
It Becomes Easier
And Easier To
Trust Others.

24. Trust

In every organization and every situation there's always one issue that comes up. Whether you're dealing with union/management, employee/ manager, teacher/student or almost any other relationship, at the bottom of every issue is trust, or the lack of it. Without trust, all the other practices and initiatives are built on a real shaky foundation.

Let's begin by defining trust. Webster's dictionary defines trust as, "assured reliance on the character, ability, strength or truth of someone or something." When we get into the issue of trust, there are some critical components that need to be discussed.

The first is that when you place trust in someone, you need to be sure they have the ability to perform the task or to carry out the function with which you've entrusted them. The term "responsibility" means the ability to respond. To place trust in someone who does not have the necessary skills or abilities will cause tremendous frustration for them and constant disappointment for you. When I work with men and women who are exiting a correctional environment, I am always aware that I need to be careful of placing trust within their capabilities of managing the responsibility. As they demonstrate trustworthiness, I'll place more and more responsibilities in their hands. This is true in dealing with any type of employee or individual. There are feedback mechanisms that allow you to measure people's progress and reduce the risks involved with trust. One thing that offers reassurance is the individual's consistency in following through on their commitments. Anytime someone follows through on something they say they're going to do, we gain confidence in that individual, including ourselves. In our workshops, we ask people to sign an agreement with themselves to commit to doing the things they need to do in order to make the changes they want. We always tell them, "Don't sign it if you don't mean it". If they commit to doing something and don't follow through, they'll lose trust in themselves. As a result, the downward spiral of negative thinking just gains momentum. If we make a commitment to others and cannot follow through, then providing feedback on the reasons for not completing the task is essential to keep trust from breaking down.

Few things help an individual more than to place responsibility upon him, and to let him know that you trust him.

                                    Booker T. Washington

Coming from a background where the absence of trust was the norm, it took many years of consistency for me to be perceived as a trustworthy individual. If a person like myself, who grew up on the streets and demonstrated illegal behavior for half of his life, can reestablish trust, then it would seem possible that trust could be developed between union/ management, departments, or individuals.

I am very careful of giving my word in areas where I cannot control the outcome. If I reach beyond my ability to influence the outcome, then I put my credibility and other's trust at risk. I was working with a plant in the south and an area manager told his employees that they would not contract out work. His commitment reached beyond his center of influence. A few short months later, the corporate leadership made a decision that forced the area manager to go back on his word. When the work was contracted out, the employees blamed the area manager. His trustworthiness was questioned by the employees, and yet the decision was made by people a thousand miles from the plant.

For organizations to maximize their abilities, there needs to be a recommitment to trust. Management needs to trust employees to do the job to the best of their abilities. Employees need to be able to trust that they can offer suggestions and ask for feedback without the risk of getting their heads chopped off. Trust starts with leadership. To establish trust we must follow through on our commitments. When we deviate from the truth, follow-through is not possible.

The foundation of any healthy relationship is trust. When trust breaks down in individuals or in organizations, subtle withdrawal behaviors occur. At first, we just stop being open in our communication. Then we begin to withhold our skills and our talents. Creativity is stifled. In relationships, we withhold our love and our affection for our partner. When trust breaks down, this withdrawal behavior can gradually and incrementally bankrupt the relationship. When we lose trust in leadership, or management, then no one wants to make a decision and everyone passes the buck. When management's trust in employees breaks down, we wind up with a hierarchical organization where we tell people what to do, how and when to do it, and then monitor their behavior closely. There is no way that I could accomplish what I do without placing tremendous trust in the people that work with me.

Children cannot grow into competent, mature adults unless they develop trustworthiness. This starts by first placing trust in the young person, allowing them to make their own decisions, even if it means giving them the opportunity to "fail" and learn from the experience. And as they demonstrate trustworthiness, we increase our trust in their ability to do the right thing. Gradually, their own self-image will include a picture of themselves as a trustworthy person, a picture they will want to live up to.

Without trust, a marital relationship will have constant conflict. When we trust ourselves and develop the consistency within ourselves, then it becomes easier and easier to trust other people. To develop trust where trust has been eroded, we need to start with a clean slate. We need to sit down and agree to certain behaviors and certain activities and then demonstrate our willingness to follow through on a consistent basis. Once we do this at the individual level, we can gradually extend it throughout the organization.

There are times when trust in an organization has been so badly eroded that it seems almost impossible to rebuild it. When that happens it's sometimes necessary to simply declare that, from here on out, we will conduct ourselves in a trustworthy manner and trust that others will do the same. This is a *simple* thing to do but not an *easy* thing to do. People have a tendency to hold on to old grievances and wear them like a suit of armor.

There were two brothers, both were monks living in a Monastery. They had taken a vow never to touch or speak to a woman for the rest of their lives. One day they were walking through the woods when they came upon a creek. There happened to be a young woman standing by the creek afraid to cross through the water. One of the brothers carried the woman across the creek. The two brothers continued to walk for several miles in complete silence. Finally, one brother could stand it no longer. He said, "Brother, we took a vow never to touch or speak to a woman for the rest of our lives and yet you carried that woman across the creek." And the other brother replied, "Yes, but I put her down. You're still carrying her."

Trust in leadership is at an all-time low in our society. It's time for us to face this issue squarely and begin to build a foundation of trust that will carry us into the next millenium. There is tremendous individual strength that comes from being trustworthy. It's a foundation you can stand on, from which to challenge unfair practices, and unfair principles. If you are not trustworthy yourself, it becomes very difficult to question other people's character.

Lessons Learned...

With Freedom Comes Responsibility - To Ourselves, And The Communities We Live In.

25.Freedom Isn't Free

Our Constitution says that we have the right to life, liberty and the pursuit of happiness. But one of the lessons that I've learned over the years is that freedom isn't free; we pay a price for it. With freedom comes responsibility. This responsibility is not just to ourselves, but to our communities and to other people as well. Freedom does not mean that we have the right to impose our will on other people or the right to impose on other people's rights. To function in a free society, people need to accept certain laws and expectations.

There's a thin line between freedom and anarchy. I've had the unfortunate experience of living in anarchy, and it is not an experience that I would choose to repeat. I finally accepted within myself that laws were necessary and it was my responsibility to operate within society's laws. If I disagree with a law or feel it is unjust, I also have a responsibility to work within the system to bring about change.

For this country to remain a free society, each of us has a responsibility to stay involved in the political process at both the national and local levels. We also have a responsibility to work aggressively to change unjust laws. When laws are passed that give the advantage to one group of people at the exclusion of others, these laws need to be questioned. When laws are unfairly administered and one segment of society suffers because of this, we need to have the courage to stand up and object.

When opportunities are made easy for one group to access, and creates a tremendous burden on another group, then we need to work for positive change. When there is an unfair distribution of wealth and the gap between the "haves" and the "have-nots" becomes so great that the have-nots are locked out of the American dream, then we need to work to modify this disparity. In an information and economic driven society, the accumulation of wealth has become easier and easier for those who have the ability and the right connections to invest, and more and more difficult for those without the economic ability and connections.

The economic gaps that currently exist in our society have evolved around race and gender. The wider the economic gap, the less freedom individuals feel. It creates a need for the "haves" to protect what they perceive as their property and forces the "have-nots" to resort to tactics that also impact freedom. Not being a student of economics or racial equality puts me somewhat at a disadvantage, but I believe that we will never resolve the racial issue unless we resolve the economic issue. We need to have equal access to opportunities and we need to find ways to bring the "have-nots" back into the mainstream.

Our freedom today is at risk because of violence and large populations of people who are disconnected from society's norms. To recapture our freedom, these issues need to be resolved.

Lessons Learned...

Without
Goals,
We
Self-Destruct.

26. Goal Setting
Is A Skill

Until I gained the wisdom that goal setting is a skill, I journeyed through life like a ball in a pinball machine, bouncing from one idea to the next. My knowledge of goal setting was gained from books, but actually experiencing the power that setting and reaching goals brought to my life gave me real wisdom.

Even if you're on the right track, you'll get run over if you just sit there.

Will Rogers

There were several different lessons on goal setting that were critical to my life on the streets. One was that the human being is goal seeking by nature. When we set a goal, our awareness opens up and we begin to gather data and information that supports and reinforces the goal.

I had never really considered goal setting beyond getting a job or getting out of prison, or getting certain needs filled. But when I became aware of two concepts that apply to goal setting, it changed my whole approach. The first was that we need to goal-set on the concept of "belief without evidence." In one of his books, Dr. Wayne Dyer states that you've got to believe before you can see. Belief without evidence suggests that we set our goals based on what we want, even though we may not know how to get there. When we set the goal, we become aware of things that we didn't see before. I accepted this principle and began to practice active goal setting. Based on my own sense of what was realistic, I began to stretch myself and set goals that, at the moment, I had no idea how to achieve. The more I practiced this technique, the more confidence I gained in its validity.

Our plans miscarry because they have no aim. When a man does not know what harbor he is making for, no wind is the right wind.
                    Seneca (4 B.C. - A.D. 65)

The other concept that had a major impact on me was the idea that without goals, we self-destruct. This was based on the belief that we seldom exceed our expectations. When I became aware of this concept, I could look back at my life and see the times that I had set a goal and, as soon as I reached it, all creative drive and energy ceased. I goal-set to get out of prison, but not to stay out. I would goal-set to escape, and be captured four days later, floundering around in the woods of Idaho, because the goal was to get out from behind The Walls, and no further. I would goal-set to get a job, but not to do it. So the idea that you must goal-set through, not to, was a tremendous awareness for me. Now, as I approach a goal, I begin to project further into the future in order to keep up the momentum.

I'd grown up in the correctional institution at Walla Walla, and when men were paroled, they usually ended up in Seattle, Washington. There is a street in Seattle called Pike Street where all of the hustlers and ex-convicts seemed to congregate. People who had goal-set to get out of prison hit Pike Street and became like a ball in a pinball machine. Someone would suggest that they go get a drink of alcohol, and their response would be, "Sounds like a good idea;" or go get a hit of dope, "Sounds like a good idea;" or go pull this caper, "Sounds like a good idea;" or go back to prison, "Sounds like a good idea." Just like a ball in a pinball machine.

When we set goals and understand the importance of the concept that we seldom exceed our expectations, it allows us to sustain ourselves through the initial target. We can goal-set to reach a contractual agreement, but not to live up to it. Or we can goal-set to get married, and never set another goal in that area of our lives, and then wonder why the marriage goes flat. We can goal-set to retire and never set another goal, and it's not long before we are among the deceased. Goal setting is a skill that has served me well in staying focused on creating and maintaining a productive, honest life.

Lessons Learned...

Belief Without
Evidence Is
At the Heart
of All
Great
Achievements.

27. Belief Without Evidence

One of the most important lessons I've learned is the value of belief without evidence in making any kind of change. It's also one of the most difficult concepts to get people to accept.

It's not hard to understand why people have such a difficult time with this concept. We live in a world where skepticism and cynicism are often necessary to protect us from shady deals and promises that are "too good to be true". We're taught that "seeing is believing". We've learned not to believe what our politicians tell us, and the once reliable media has turned into an unreliable mix of soundbites and sensational one-liners. "Don't believe anything you hear and only half of what you see", we're warned.

Most of the time, this is good advice. However, when we're trying to make changes in our personal lives and our organizations, the willingness to believe that change is possible can be one of our biggest challenges. It's not that we don't want the change to happen, it's just that we have overwhelming evidence, based on what's happened in the past, that nothing and nobody ever really changes for very long.

At this point, we come to a crossroads where we have two choices: we either give up the possibility of making change, or we decide to go ahead and believe change is possible without the evidence.

Belief without evidence is at the heart of all great achievements. It goes against logic and enters the realm of the spiritual. Belief without evidence opens the mind to all possibilities and we begin to cluster resources that seem to appear as if by magic.

When I first became aware of this nebulous concept, my reaction was, "yeah, right". But what I've learned since then is that all knowledge and all information already exists; we are just rediscovering it. So, when we set a goal, the mind automatically opens to information that supports the goal. Someone said "you've got to believe before you can see". One of our greatest challenges is to recognize our own abilities and our potential as individuals. We limit ourselves by the way we think and one of our self-imposed limitations is rooted in our need to know the "how" prior to setting a goal.

Belief without evidence is not some pie-in-the-sky idea that suggests that all you need to do is have the belief and the rest will take care of itself. You still have to put your energy and skills to work, but the process of believing creates opportunities and awareness that help you achieve your goal. This, in turn, creates some *new* evidence about what's possible.

There are thousands of stories of people who have started with a belief that they could make a difference and their belief became the cornerstone of this great country. Now we need to approach the next millenium with a new belief that we can create a world that offers hope, opportunities, and equality to all people.

Life has been an exciting journey for me. It's taken many twists and turns to finally wind up where I am today. There's many things I would do differently if I could go back and do them over again. But that's not an option so I'll continue to play the hand I've been dealt to the best of my ability.

I want to be a voice for positive change. I want to work to provide options and opportunities for men and women caught up in prisons, both mentally and physically. I want to reach out to young people and help build a bridge to a future filled with peace and prosperity. I want to work toward a society where racism exists only in the history books. I want to see a time when labor and management understands that there's only one path to survival and that path is a win/win relationship. Damn, wouldn't that be a goal we could *all* get excited about?

I don't have evidence that it's possible to achieve all these goals, but I choose to believe it is.

Epilogue

Walla Walla is Washington State's maximum security prison, commonly referred to as the "Walls." This was the place that formed and molded so much of who I am and what I have become. The huge cellblocks, the big yard, Big Red, and the maximum security building all left deep, unforgettable impressions in my mind. Before I could bring closure to this book, I knew I had to revisit this prison that still haunts my memories.

It's been years since I've been inside the Walls. I've avoided it like the plague. I'm in prisons every month all across the United States and Canada: Folsom, San Quentin, Leavenworth, some of the toughest prisons in the country. But Walla Walla is different. I grew up behind those walls. For years I lived in a four-man cell, with a toilet and sink attached to the back of the cell, stripped of all privacy and human dignity. I was living in 13-B six-wing when President Kennedy was assassinated and the Korean War was fought. When man first walked on the moon I was walking the big yard. My son was born in downtown Walla Walla while I was serving time. When my prison experience finally ended, my life was tightly wrapped by years of yard out, chow line, count time, lights out, and the constant awareness that I was a convict.

Since I left The Walls twenty-seven years ago, I've totally changed the picture of who I am. But there's still an anxiety when I think about going back to revisit Walla Walla. There was something in me that didn't want to flood my head with memories of those wasted years of confinement. I didn't want to see the faces of men that I'd served time with who are still locked behind bars. I didn't want to inter-act with the prison guards who had been my keep-ers. I didn't want to experience the humiliation that goes along with visiting prisons. It didn't bother me so much in other institutions, but I had experienced enough humiliation in Walla Walla to last a lifetime. In spite of all this, I knew I had to go back before this book could be complete.

It was Friday morning, May 22, 1998. Four of us drove from Seattle to Walla Walla the night be-fore. We were due up on "The Hill" (a slang term for the prison) at 8:30 a.m. I'd brought reinforce-ment with me to help ease the anxiety of going back inside the Walls. My wife Eve, David Lewis, Guy Kurose, and Cathy Crosslin, had all agreed to visit the joint with me. They knew that I was out of my comfort zone. I'd been to Walla Walla a number of times after I was first released, but it had been years since I'd been back. I knew there had been major changes at the Walls, but I couldn't have imagined what I was about to see.

We drove the short distance to the prison and

parked in the visitors' parking area. The five of us walked up the sidewalk and into the prison. We cleared the metal detectors and were processed through the security checkpoints. The walls were a different color and the area where you entered the prison was all new. We were met by a young woman from the Education Department who had been facilitating our video training series, *Breaking Barriers*. A lady at the desk checked off our names. Our driver's licenses were exchanged for visitor passes and our left hands were stamped with ink that is visible only under a fluorescent light. Without the stamp you don't get back out! *I wanted a heavy dose of ink on my hand!*

Our first stop was the Education Department where we were to speak to a group of inmates. There was room for about 80 people, and we spent an hour talking about change and how to take control of your life. Men and women in prison are the same all across America. The majority will be getting out of prison and returning to their communities. It's critical that we do something during their incarceration that will give them some chance of returning to their communities better equipped to succeed than when they were sentenced. Change is an inside job, but we need to give people tools to bring about lasting change. My message is always the same. We are all accountable for our own lives. That's the first step to change. Second, there is a body of knowledge that, when properly applied, can change your life. Most men and women have the potential to get out of prison and stay out. There needs to be more attention paid to the process of change. We tend to build a half-mile bridge across a mile-wide river. We need to extend the bridge from what happens during incarceration to what happens when the person returns to the streets.

When we finished the presentation to the inmates, one of the staff members agreed to take us on a tour of the prison. He asked me what I wanted to see. The prison had been totally restructured. I'd lived for years inside these walls and I was lost! I asked to see the six and eight wings (the cellblocks where I'd spent most of my time), the big yard, Blood Alley, and the auditorium. These were areas that impacted my life while I was an inmate. He said, "Blood Alley is gone, and the auditorium isn't there anymore." Blood Alley was a stretch of sidewalk that you traveled to reach the auditorium. The prison hospital on one side, and 6-wing on the other, created a blind spot where you were out of sight of gun towers and prison guards. Stabbings and assaults were common occurrences on Blood Alley.

"Let's go over to six-wing," I said. For some reason, I wanted to see the cellblock that I lived in when Kennedy was shot. The prison had been sectioned off with fences and new buildings. The red brick walls had been covered with a dull gray cement and the whole atmosphere seemed lifeless. Inmates hurried by the guard with their eyes to the ground, or with a quick sideways glance. Occasionally a small group interacted with us and tried to strike up a conversation with Eve or Cathy.

When we reached six-wing, a corrections officer opened the steel door and allowed us to enter. Six-wing is a huge cellblock with four-man cells. There are sixteen cells on each tier, and it's three tiers high. The top tier is an oven during the hot sweltering months of summer. I'd lived in 13-B on the bottom tier. When I looked down the tier, the memories rushed through my body. Locked in a ten-foot by eleven-foot cubicle with three other grown men. All of your worldly possessions crammed in footlockers. The noise and smells dominate your senses and the Man's got the key. I didn't hear the constant "key up," which was the inmates' way of getting released from the cell back when I was doing time. But, the cells hadn't changed. Two double-bunks, one on each side of the cell. The space between the bunks allowed access to the back of the cell where the sink and toilet were located. Usually the cell had a table and chair in one corner that inmates could use for writing letters or for card games. There was only room for one person to pace the floor, so if the cell had two pacers, you had to do it in shifts. I couldn't imagine how I'd survived those years. Today I need space and privacy. When I use the bathroom, I lock the door even if my wife and I are the only ones in the house. Now I know why I love the mountains and rivers of Montana, where you can see for miles and the air is sweet and clean.

I looked down the long row of cells to 13-B and the words "key up" rattled through my mind. I wanted out. I turned to our escort and said, "Let's get out of here." But a piece of me still reaches out to people who are locked up in prisons. Have they ever experienced the freedom of Montana? The joy of feeling whole? The peace that comes from being in control of your own life? The ability to make your own decisions? To love unconditionally and to live an open and honest existence? The ability to use the bathroom in private and have the key to the door?

Our next stop was the big yard. The guard in the gun tower that overlooks the yard pulled the lever that opens the metal door, allowing us to enter the yard. The big yard, like the rest of the prison, had changed. It was bare. The old recreation shack was gone, the bleachers were gone, the ball field didn't exist. It was a stark prison yard; a huge barren space. I remembered the football games, the boxing cards, the baseball teams that brought a degree of excitement to the joint. There were bleachers outside the walls so people from the outside could watch the ball games and prize fights. On the Fourth of July and Labor Day, we set up a boxing ring on the pitcher's mound and scheduled a fight card. The outside bleachers filled with people from downtown Walla Walla. Inside the Walls, the inmates settled into makeshift seats and spread out across the dusty infield to witness these events. I'd fought some wars in the hundred-degree temperatures of a Walla Walla summer. The big yard offered a release. You could walk the yard and escape the insanity of prison life. The fights and the games gave inmates an opportunity to use their skills and to let off steam. For an afternoon you felt normal. When you put on your athletic gear, you became a ball player or a fighter. Your number was on your uniform, not on your prison record.

Now, all of this was gone. The yard was a sterile, lifeless space of cement and dirt. The walls were gray, and on one wall there was a long row of telephones. It was more like an industrial yard than a prison. "Damn, this is a different world," I thought as I gazed at the area above the walls where the bleachers used to be.

I didn't like the feeling that was stirring in my being. The whole structure was designed around control. It was like the humanness was gone. What happened to the characters that made up Walla Walla? The Whitey Norman's, a nondescript little man with thick-framed glasses and wispy gray hair, who believed he drove the chain car, the bus that brought new inmates to Walla Walla. Whitey would tell me about the latest load of convicts he'd brought in and how he'd had to get tough with a couple of punks. I'd mess with Whitey by telling him that Joe, a partner of mine, said that Whitey didn't drive the chain car, that Joe did. Whitey would get angry and cuss Joe out, "That S.O.B., I'm going to kick his ass. I drive the chain car, you ask the warden." Whitey was a couple of pickles short of a jar! But he was harmless and I liked the old guy. I never knew why he was in prison, but there was no other place for people like Whitey at that time. Then there was an inmate named Vern. He was a tall sallow-faced individual who never talked. He was always picking imaginary bugs off his arms. He carried a roll of newspapers in his back pocket and would stand and pick at the bugs. Then he would wash his hands over and over and then go back to his newspaper and his bugs. He was standing in one of the old cellblocks that had been gutted and turned into a recreation area one evening during recreation time; his newspapers stuffed in his pockets, picking at his arms. Suddenly he unbuttoned his pants, pulled out his penis, took a ruler from his pocket and measured his penis. He put the ruler back in his pocket, buttoned his pants, and went back to picking, as though his actions were as normal as could be. At first I was stunned, and then I laughed until my sides ached. There was another inmate who thought he was a motorcycle. He could make a noise that sounded just like a Harley Davidson. I'm sure these guys belonged in a mental institution, but they were a part of Walla Walla's culture.

This sterile, controlled environment didn't seem to have a place for the old characters that made up the prison where I'd done my time. There was nothing familiar about the Walls. I didn't have to see anymore. We stopped by the mess hall on our way out. It was lunchtime and the chow hall was full. I remembered the years that I'd sat at the same table for breakfast, lunch and dinner. I didn't want to stay in the mess hall long. I remembered how I hated having outsiders watch me when I was a convict. It made you feel like you were an animal in a zoo. "Let's go out to the minimum security building," I suggested to the group.

We left the inside of the Walls and caught a van that carried us to the minimum security building. This was where I'd served my last few months in prison. My wife and children had visited me there. This was where I'd first begun to consider the idea of staying out of prison.

The changes inside the Walls were nothing compared to the changes at the minimum security building. It was now considered medium security, but the high razor wire fences and the gray cement housing units called "pods" gave the impression of a space age prison complex. Again, it was all about systems designed around control. The staff was friendly, and the inmates seemed to follow the structured routine with minimal resistance. But the opportunity to learn responsibility and decision-making didn't seem to exist. When I was in the minimum security building, there were no fences. You had to accept responsibility and you were forced to make some difficult choices. But it helped prepare me for the streets. Where and how does the inmate face these challenges today? Or have we given up on the process of change only to dump men and women back into society with little or no chance of success?

The old five-hole golf course the inmates had designed was gone. An industrial building now occupied the space that had been the first tee-off. A pig farm used to set off to the right of the first tee. If an inmate sliced his drive, it could land in the pigpen. Some golf balls had liquid centers in those days and if a pig ate a ball, it could kill the pig. This was not good, because if that happened, the inmate would be sent back inside the Walls! So if an inmate sliced off that first tee, you would see him racing for the pigpen to beat the pig to the ball. It was not unusual to see an inmate wrestling a pig for a golf ball! The greens were sand and the rough was very rough, but it allowed inmates to participate in a game that teaches self-discipline. By the time you reached minimum, you had been thoroughly punished and were on your way out of the joint. It was time to start adjusting to the real world. I didn't play golf, but I always thought it was a positive for the inmates who did.

We were scheduled to speak to a group of inmates in the minimum security building. An old friend of mine who has served thirty-two consecutive years in prison asked me if I would talk to the men there. He had been in prison with me and we have remained in contact over the past twenty-six years. I was scheduled to speak in the gym, so it made it possible for more people to participate.

A couple of hundred inmates showed up for our presentation and, to my surprise, there were several who had been there when I was serving time. They were older and the wear and tear of life had taken its toll, but we knew each other from another time and place. They brought back old memories from the past. They reminded me of the time I'd stopped a race riot inside The Walls and of other experiences that are now buried in the archives of my mind. A young man asked me to look at his nametag, and then said, "Do you remember this name?" I couldn't and told him so. He then pulled out a picture from his pocket and said, "Do you remember him?" I vaguely seemed to recall the face. He then said, "That was my dad. I never knew him. I need to know who he was." The young man's eyes pleaded with me to know something of his father who had been in prison with me. The only thing I could say was, "I think he was a good guy, a stand-up kind of guy, who did his own time." He needed to know his dad was an okay guy, but I couldn't remember the man whose son was now in the Walls. My son was born when I was serving my last prison sentence. I'd been allowed to go from the minimum security building to the hospital where Gordy was born to see my wife and baby boy. Gordy will turn twenty-seven on July 11, 1998. He's a good young man, and we're good friends as well as father and son. He is now a father with a daughter and son (the third Gordon Graham). The cycle can be broken. It saddens me when I see the sons and daughters of inmates behind bars.

The day at Walla Walla left me drained. To see our prisons move toward an industrial-like complex is a scary thing. I recognize the need for control and order, but there needs to be a recognition that we are dealing with human beings. To create automated systems that turn men and women into non-thinking products has a dehumanizing effect on an individual.

The prison on the hill provides some of the best paying jobs in Walla Walla. The benefits are good and the jobs offer long-term security. The measurement of whether we do a good job or not is basically about control. There's no real emphasis on an inmate's chances of staying out, but rather how they adjust to the systems of control. Does conforming to an abnormal environment prepare you for the real world? I think not. Walla Walla is probably a typical correctional complex. But it's different for me. There's so much of who I am that was developed behind The Walls. It's hard to accept the decision society has made regarding public safety. We have developed technology that challenges the limits of our imagination and yet our prison systems remain in the Dark Ages. We have digressed from a correctional system that showed signs of success in changing behavior to a sophisticated system of maximum control with longer and longer periods of incarceration; a system driven more and more by economics, with big business determining correctional decisions. Prisons have become huge warehouse-like structures built in unpopulated areas or in areas where industrial jobs have dried up and the prison brings jobs to the community. But when you visit a prison and talk to men and women who are caught up in this system, you realize how costly it will be long-term. It will eventually bankrupt society. There must be a better way.

I'm glad I visited Walla Walla. I found the correctional staff much more considerate than I had expected. The changes kept me from getting emotionally hooked, because it's a different world today. It has brought me full circle. I'm free of the Walls and the humiliation of being a prisoner. Washington State is no better or worse than other states where I work. The men and women who staff the prisons are caught up in the system the same as the inmates. The taxpayer has somehow decided that they will finance an industrial complex where the product is human beings. The larger it gets, the harder it is to change. Our streets are much more dangerous than ever before in history. Serious crimes are being committed by younger and younger children. These problems did not develop in prisons, the crimes were not hatched behind The Walls. Pouring more and more of our tax dollars into steel bars, razor wire and technology to control men and women in prison will do nothing to solve these problems.

Today we have thousands upon thousands of men and women who are serving astronomically long prison terms who could turn their lives around and become productive members of society. We know what works for these offenders. We have sound data that demonstrates the success rate, and yet we continue to lock them up in maximum security prisons. It's estimated that at least 80% of incarcerated prisoners have a drug or alcohol problem that contributed to their crime. This does not excuse the crime, nor am I suggesting that punishment should not be a part of the consequences. But to lock a person away for 10, 15 or 20 years, makes no sense. Treatment works! Punishment, treatment, and follow-through would save taxpayers millions of dollars every year that could be diverted to families and schools in dire need of assistance.

My trip to Walla Walla had an alarming impact on me as a citizen. I became aware of just how far we've moved toward treating corrections as an industry. Businesses, from phone companies to manufacturing plants, from food suppliers to paper products, to the tax base of communities, have gradually become dependent on prisons. We've created a situation that demands more and more bodies to fill the cells. This means that some segment of society needs to be locked up. The incentive to change or correct behavior becomes a mute voice in a fear-driven, media-based information age. There are more successes than failures; but success doesn't make the news and inmates can't vote.

Walla Walla will always be a part of my memories. But the Walls that I knew no longer exist. The characters have disappeared. The treatment programs and therapies are still there, but they seem plastic, with no passion to change the world. The joint seems roboticized with humanness drained from its pores. Maybe I'm just getting old, but damn, I'd take the days when, even though the joint was tough, there was a humanness about it and people still believed that change was possible. *I know change is possible.*

The Bridge Builder

An old man going down a lone highway
Came in the evening cold and gray
To a chasm vast and deep and wide
Through which was flowing a sullen-tide.
The old man crossed in the twilight dim;
That swollen stream held no fears for him;
But he turned when safe on the other side
And built a bridge to span the tide.

"Old man," said a fellow pilgrim near,
"You are wasting your strength with building here;
Your journey will end with the ending day;
You never again must pass this way;
You have crossed the chasm deep and wide-
Why build you this bridge at the eventide?"

The builder lifted his old gray head
"Good friend, in the path I have come," he said,
"There followeth after me today
A youth whose feet must pass this way.
This swollen stream which was naught to me
To that fair-haired youth may a pitfall be;
He, too, must cross in the twilight dim;
Good friend, I am building the bridge for him."

Author Unknown

An Invitation to Our Readers . . .

If you have a story of change or transformation you'd like to share, please send it to us. Or if we've inspired you to recall one of your own Lessons Learned, let us know. Together we can continue to learn, to grow, and make the world a better place.

Our address is:

Gordon Graham & Company
2630 - 116th Avenue, N.E., Suite 102
Bellevue, WA 98004

Or

Mail@ggco.com